An illustrate

PORT

"One of the least spoiled and most impressive
of Cornish fishing villages."

Sir John Betjeman

Keith Johns & Mike Rule

2004

Acknowledgement

The Authors would especially like to thank all those villagers who have given freely and enthusiastically of their memories and their photographs. For his help and advice on the writings of Charles Lee we are indebted to Simon Parker, and for help generally we wish to thank and acknowledge The Cornwall Centre at Redruth, The Royal Institution of Cornwall and the Cornwall County Record Office. We would like to thank the latter two organisations for allowing us to use some additional photographs. Every effort has been made to contact authors and we apologise to those we have failed to trace. We will be happy to correct any omissions in future editions.

Keith Johns & Mike Rule

Portloe - An Illustrated History

First edition published 2004

Published by:
Palores Publishing
Redruth, Kernow

Designed & Printed by:
St Ives Printing & Publishing Company
High Street, St Ives, Cornwall TR26 1RS, U.K.

ISBN 0-9547985-4-6

CONTENTS

INTRODUCTION

Portloe has been a settlement for many hundreds of years. Certainly documented in Tudor times, its origins are probably much earlier. In Queen Elizabeth's reign (the mid to late sixteenth century) every cove in Cornwall '*had its "palace" or curing cellar. Even between the cliffs where but a small patch of sand was available, and this covered at high tide, rocks were hewn away and levelled to establish a "palace" or "place". The fishing villages along the South coast became mere collections of fish cellars, with the fishers' dwellings on top. In the cellars were stored nets, salt and fish in the process of cure. It is interesting to note that old parchments describe fishing village houses as "palaces".*' (1). Portloe would have exactly fitted this description.

In a survey of fishermen of 1626 Veryan Parish had eight, without doubt living in and working from Portloe. (2). It was during the seventeenth and eighteenth centuries that the Cornish fishing industry really began to develop. Just as Cornish mining was primarily identified with tin, so Cornish fishing was primarily identified with the pilchard. Portloe owes its existence to fish and fishing, and it is to the humble pilchard (*Sardina pilchardus*) that we should look for the beginnings and subsequent development of this remarkably self-reliant fishing village.

Its position at the centre of the sweep of water known as Veryan Bay, nestling between the protective headlands of the Dodman and the Nare Head would have been ideal for early pilchard fishermen. Sheltered and secluded it is a natural small haven where light craft could be hauled safely above high water mark and launched in most sea conditions.

Stone was in abundance from the cliff face for building. The steep sided valleys provided shelter from the worst of the weather as well as timber from the trees. Clean water was available from both streams and springs. These are the reasons for the settlement's foundation.

Although there was probably a small community here in the late Middle Ages, the houses belong to a later time. Early attempts at house-building would have been crude and of short-lived construction and would have long since disappeared. The earliest houses that survive today, built around the cove, date from the late seventeenth century and were erected on the sites of the less durable residences. The early homes, built of stone and cob, were very basic and consisted of a living room with fish cellar below or adjoining at the side.

A South Wales collier waits for the tide to ebb so that it may unload onto the beach. The cultivated fields, unlike those of today, allow us to see the old road out of Portloe to the West snaking along the hillside. c1912

Houses were leased from the Squire, not always for a definite term of years, but often for the duration of the longest of three select lives; or, a nominal 99 years, determinable on the death of the last survivor of the persons nominated in the document.

The present day cottages, built over a period of some two hundred years are a tribute to generations of unknown architects and craftsmen who worked out the problems of house construction for themselves. It is the humanity behind the stones that is the basis for our story. This book hopes to inform and entertain the reader with Portloe's history through highs and lows of population, trade and tourism. Like all small communities many families have dominated and the reader will soon identify such surnames as Johns, Blamey, Dunstone and Trudgeon as regularly appearing over the years. Charles Lee, who we will encounter later, described Portloe's population as '*an intricate net of cross-relationships tangling us all up in a way that would make the most expert of genealogists tear his hair out.*'(3).

Portloe is in the Parish of Veryan and for a history of the wider area we strongly recommend the excellent *The Parish of Veryan* written by Christine North and republished in 1996. Christine, a former County Archivist, lives nearby at Camels.

(1) *Cornwall Education Week Handbook,* Cornwall C C. 1927

(2) PRO SP 16/34/98, 103 Survey of Fishermen, 1626

(3) Charles Lee, *Cornish Tales,* Dent 1941

Richard Blamey Johns (*Deaf Dick*) with his son Fred alongside their typical Portloe fishing boat. The hand-barrow on the sand is a gurry. A common expression In Portloe for a handy amount is a *"gurry lod (load)"*

"Some leaning over the side of a boat intently staring at her bottom." Lee. A photograph taken by Joseph Greet c1900 of Malachi Blamey, Edward Dunstone, William Soper and Benjamin Dunstone

FISHING
PORTLOE'S FOUNDATION

The great mainstay of the fishing trade for centuries up to the mid nineteenth was a fish smaller than a herring and larger than its juvenile stage the sardine, the pilchard. From the Atlantic it reached the Cornish coast in mid July, remaining in coastal waters until November or December. For nearly all of Cornwall's inhabitants the pilchard was the staple diet, eaten fresh in the summer and salted down for winter. During August look-outs were posted on cliff vantage points after news of the pilchards' arrival in West Cornwall quickly spread. In Portloe 'Watch Rock', up on the Downs beyond The Jacka, was a favoured spot. The look-out, or 'huer' (probably deriving from the Cornish word 'hevva' – a shoal of fish) armed with a furze bush, or similar, would watch for a dark shadow on the sea, indicating to his experienced eye a shoal of pilchards. Meanwhile boats, nets and men would be waiting. The huer would indicate, firstly by calling "hevva" through a large trumpet, and then by a simple form of semaphore with the furze to the fishermen the direction in which the shoal was going. The boats were launched and the seine net was shot with the object being to entrap the entire shoal of hundreds of thousands of fish. Three boats made up a typical Portloe seining company, the 'stop' boat, rowed by six men and carrying the massive main net of up to 400 yards long; the following boat of similar size which carried the 'tuck' net, and lastly the 'lurker' from which the head of the seine directed operations. The shoal was encircled by the main seine net. Capstans on the boat were used to haul the net tightly together and nearer to the shore. The fish were then taken from within the seine net by repeated shootings of the smaller 'tuck' seine.

Back on shore the next procedure was to get the pilchards into carts or barrows to the salting houses where the women and children layered them in salt. This process, called baulking, meant building a wall of fish three feet high and two feet wide. For about thirty days the pilchards would remain in baulk. Apart from those for local consumption, the rest were washed and carefully packed into hogsheads (a barrel of about 50 gallons containing

Father and son, both named Jospeh Trudgeon, Great-grandfather and Grandfather of Joey and Ron Trudgeon with a thresher shark caught in 1905

about 3,000 fish) layer upon layer, tails to the centre. When full, a lid called a buckler was placed on top with a weighted pole continually pressing the fish. More and more pilchards would be added until the barrel was full. The oil that ran out of the cask was gullied into a pot. This 'train oil' was used to fuel the 'pilchard chills' which for centuries lit Portloe's cottages.

There was little demand for pilchards in England, but in Italy, Spain and to a lesser extent The West Indies there was a need to satisfy the strict religious observance. Harris in 1906 recounts somewhat cynically *'that it showed a fine spirit to feed poor benighted Italians who crossed themselves, and pouch a hundred thousand sterling a year for the trouble. Pickled pilchards he looked on as a bond of union between the two countries. Pilchards feed bodies, the Pope souls and the shekels come here. Long live the pilchard!*

"Here's to the health of the Pope! May he live to repent,
And add just six months to the term of his Lent,
And tell all his vassals from Rome to the Poles,
There's nothing like pilchards for saving their souls." (1).

The seine was a form of co-operative fishing with each member able to combine labour, boats and suitable nets to accomplish the task. Portloe had three or more seines in the eighteenth century. In 1753 the seine of John Luke and partners built a fish cellar, probably in the area that is now The Lugger Hotel car park. In 1778 a plot of land was leased for a cellar by the shareholders of the *Favourite* seine. (2). The same offering three boats for sale in June 1812. Although the quantity of fish caught varied from year to year, sometimes there being none, twenty hogsheads were in one seine at Pendower in 1801, while the following year saw one hundred hogsheads, while another had enclosed an immense shoal. Unfortunately the net gave way and all but twenty-five hogsheads escaped.

Taken in August 1911 showing the two larger seine boats near the top of the slip.

The pilchard catch was subject to a Church tithe or tax. Once rendered in kind, such a practice became inconvenient and instead a money levy was introduced. A survey of 1836 showed that one twelfth of the mens' share shall be paid at Portloe. (3). But following many years of poor catches the tithe lapsed.

An example of co-operation took place in October 1839. '*One of the seines belonging to this place (Portloe) was shot in Gerrans Bay and watched by the crew of another seine, and when the shot seine was half-hauled up, the other crew, suspecting that a bungling affair was likely, shot their seine round them. The first took five hogsheads and the watchful party got nearly seventeen hogsheads as a reward for their industry, showing that a good shoal is frequently lost from want of proper management.*' (4). The report does not mention how the catch was shared!

In September 1856 James Blamey's seine *Concord* secured thirty-five hogsheads of pilchards, another seine landed a few mauns (baskets) of chad (young bream), but the strong tide carried a third seine net onto the rocks and tore it, missing a large shoal. (5).

Seining was in decline by the 1860's. The immense shoals were becoming smaller and appeared less frequently. The fishermen blamed the growth of

The three boats are *May Blossom*, *Mona* and *Zona*. The fishermen include Jack Trudgeon, Fred Trudgeon and Cyril Johns. The building in the middle background is an air-raid shelter

the drift fishery whose miles of nets caught or broke up the shoals way off shore. Others blamed a change in the Gulf Stream affecting the pilchard's migration routes.

The skills of the Portloe fishermen were recognised in 1872 when a seine was formed at Harlyn, near Padstow named The Cataclew Fishing Company. Cellars and lofts were built, boats constructed and nets procured. But because of the lack of expertise seiners from Gorran Haven and Portloe were hired to shoot the new net on October 13th. (6).

With the pilchard becoming less common, mackerel seining continued for a time. But the fish was difficult to preserve and this fishery never reached the heights of the pilchard industry.

The lot of the Portloe fisherman, as well as those elsewhere, is one of which he is least in control. Depending upon tide, weather, sea condition and season he uses his own vessel, equipment and skill to obtain a product that will produce a return at a level which is determined by the market. While at sea the fisherman, alone or one of a pair, concentrates on little else than the job in hand. He hopes for a catch rich in quantity of a species that is in demand. But in reality his livelihood depends on the middlemen that fix the prices. If catches are plentiful, down of course goes the price. If catches however are scarce a rising price will not compensate for the extra time and fuel required to obtain a diminishing resource. Fishing was and is subject to fluctuation, both in the prices obtained and in the quantity of fish taken, tending to make the fisherman's livelihood a precarious and uncertain one.

The Census of 1851 records 38 fishermen working in Portloe and that of 1891 showing 53. It is interesting to note that a Cornish Commission on fishing in 1861 officially recorded only 29. Perhaps when completing the Census form to write fisherman in the occupation column may conceal a less active working life due to age or an enforced lay-off owing to a lack of fish. At that time, 1861, pilchards were scarce with hake and haddock few in number. The predominant fishery was for conger, using a boulter - a line some 450 fathoms long with 300 hooks - that lay on the seabed. This method would also catch dogfish, cod and ling. Charles Lee visiting Portloe in 1898 observed about 50 boats, almost one to each man (comparing almost exactly with the 1891 Census), but as they mostly went out two to a boat, half the boats were usually laid up. He also observed that the fishing territories were not sacrosanct to each port. Gorran men fish off Portloe and Mevagissey, Mevagissey men off Gorran, Portloe men off Gorran and Falmouth. He noted too the attitude taken by the Portloe fishermen while at leisure on the beach, an attitude that the modern observer may draw a parallel with. '*Some (fishermen) leaning over the side of a boat, intently staring at her bottom. Another standing with his back to everybody else gazing up town. Others, sitting on timber or ground. Nobody looking at anybody else. The result when they are talking to a stranger who does not know the voices is a curious ventriloquial effect. All the voices seem to come from one person - which person one cannot tell.*'

His Journal entry for 21st October 1898 saw a good catch of plaice, forty score between five boats. One boat had twelve and a half score, an unprecedented number, eight score is considered good. (7).

Flat fish like plaice, sole and turbot were often caught by spiltering or trammelling. The former having 300 hooks and baited with cuttle or whatever could be found. The trammel was a small net, one-man operated from a rowing boat. The net was suspended from floats and weighted with stones.

The 1930 pilchard season was described as "an utter failure", the worst for fifty years, catches of white fish were also poor. Yet in that year the landing of the boats engaged in the crab fishery exceeded those of the corresponding season for ten years past. (8). The crabber hauled dozens of pots a day by hand, hoping for crab and lobster of a saleable size. The pots were constructed from withy stems, the willows being grown in small withy gardens wherever a small plot of ground near a stream could be found. Each pot would be baited with whatever could be found. '*They say in Portloe*', wrote Lee, '*that sharks make good bait, they smill (smell) that wild, terrible wild sharks do smill!*' (9).

Improvements to Portloe's harbour were considered at various times in the village's history. A major report containing an impressive and progressive plan for the construction of two piers was put forward in the '*Portloe Harbour Order 1917*'. This Order laid down various procedures of management including that of raising revenue, the registering of fishermen and the powers to dredge. It also put forward in great detail a proposed pier-building programme. Designed by Civil Engineer W T Douglas, it advised the construction of a South Pier (or breakwater) 180 feet long by 31 feet wide with a clearance of only 6 inches above high water at spring tides! An approach road of 200 feet in length and 20 feet wide would be constructed commencing at the East side of the School House. A second North Pier would be constructed from a point on the North side of the cove 100 feet West of the existing Coastguard slipway. Running in a SSE direction, it would incorporate Caddy Daw rock and be of 160 feet in length and just 3 feet wide. Approximately 1,100 cubic yards of rock and boulders would be removed from the harbour bed, much of which would be used, together with sand from the cove to provide aggregate for the concrete. The total cost of the entire project was estimated to be £5,100 - this factor alone would appear to be the reason why the constructions were never made, despite support being promised from the Cornwall Sea Fisheries District.

After the Second World War local feeling was once again looking towards harbour improvements. With two piers still in mind the fishermen again explained the difficulties with wind and tide affecting the hours that they could work. Plans were once again drawn up for a two pier construction costing some £16,500, but there were still doubts over the protection afforded

Leslie '*Tim*' Johns, Fred Trevarton, Joey Trudgeon, Fred Trudgeon, Cyril Johns and Jack Trudgeon in 1955

Cyril Johns, author Keith's father, with a large store-pot in the 60's

from the SE winds. Mr.W Carter, Engineer of The Ministry of War Transport visited Portloe in August 1944 to meet the fishermen and to see the situation for himself. He concluded that *"the small number of vessels using Portloe, its unsuitable natural position and the fact that the fishing industry there has been on the decline for many years, make it impossible to recommend the expenditure of the relatively large sum necessary to improve the Harbour, however sympathetic one may feel towards the local residents who are dependant on fishing for their livelihood."* Not surprisingly the piers were not built.

Concerns over the harbour were voiced by Sir Arthur Booth who lived at Shag Rock. *The West Briton* of 25th August 1949 reported that *"The need for good harbour facilities at Portloe were stressed by Sir Arthur when he opened a Gala Day."* The report noted the desire to build a 'jetty'.

Team work in carrying the mauns. James Henry, Billy Moore, Ron Trudgeon, Leslie '*Tim*' Johns, William Arthur Blamey and Henry Johns

Changing beach levels caused concern in the 40's and 50's with a shingle drop of between 2 and 3 feet at the end of the slipway. Improvements were made in 1951 with an extension being added to the original 1925 slip. Later in 1959 the breakwater (pier) that we see today was constructed at an approximate cost of £4,200, a part of which was left in his will by Tom Blamey.

Today the crab and lobster industry employs three or so fishermen. In favourable conditions each winching a hundred or so pots a day. The last ten to fifteen years has seen a fifty per cent drop in the number of Portloe's professional fishermen.

An early form of stock conservation was the bi-product of a ban on fishing in Falmouth Bay during the Second World War. After many years of being unfished, Cyril Johns told me, that once back, the crab and lobster catches were amazing in both size and quality. Of course, after a few years things returned to normal.

Joey and Ron Trudgeon typified the traditional set-up at Portloe. After leaving school Joey worked with his uncle until in 1954, with brother Ron, they made use of a Government grant of £560 to purchase their own boat 'Olga'. They fished from this trusty craft for nearly fifty years in the time-honoured method of double manning. One of their regular fishing areas was that near The Dodman – often inhospitable and not too popular. During the winter months they would construct about one hundred withy pots for the following season.

On shore, Cyril Johns and Joey Trudgeon. Afloat, Jack and Ronnie Trudgeon and William Arthur Blamey with Leslie *Tim* Johns

(1) J Henry Harris, *Cornish Saints & Sinners*, The Bodley Head 1906
(2) C North, *The Parish of Veryan*, Veryan Parochial Church Council 1996
(3) C Noall, *Cornish Seines & Seiners*, Bradford Barton 1972
(4) *The West Briton* 11th October 1839
(5) C Noall
(6) C Noall
(7) K C Phillipps, ed. *The Cornish Journal of Charles Lee*, Tabb House 1995
(8) *The West Briton* 18th December 1930
(9) K C Phillipps

WRECK, WRECKING & RESCUE

The bays of Veryan and Gerrans have seen their fair share of shipwrecks. Their proximity to the busy port of Falmouth and to the commercial shipping lanes meant that vessels of all sizes had to pass quite closely. In severe weather, adverse winds or periods of very poor visibility a captain could easily find himself a few fateful miles from the safety of Falmouth Bay. To the west of Falmouth lies Lizard Point and the treacherous Manacle Reefs, and to the east the hazards of the Nare Head with its Gull Rock and the mighty Dodman. On this coast between these imposing headlands, hidden in a tiny inlet, lies Portloe.

In December 1830 the newly built brig *Bacchus* ran onto the Gull Rock being lost with all hands. In the same month violent winds drove three ships ashore near Portholland. The French schooner *La Mayenne*, the Danish galliot *Catherine Margaretta* and the Russian brig *Saint Nicholas* all grounded some distance from the shore, each breaking up very quickly. Luckily a boat from the *Saint Nicholas* washed ashore relatively undamaged. Five young fishermen put off to the wrecks with little thought for their own safety. '*They first saved the ten crew of the* Saint Nicholas, *and then the seven from the* La Mayenne. *The crew of the* Catherine Margaretta *also got safely ashore, but by what means is not recorded.*' (1). The Royal Cornwall Gazette gave a description of the rescue, '*Too much praise cannot be given to the fishermen of Port Holland Bay. They stripped to their drawers, not withstanding the weather was piercing cold, and after great toil and at the imminent hazard of their lives, they succeeded in getting a boat near enough to effect their object an act of heroism worthy of British sailors.*' (2). However the local populace saw no problem with the moral dichotomy that ensued. The morning after the selfless heroism of the rescue the 'wrecking' instinct took over. The Royal Cornwall Gazette reported, '*On the following day the country people came down to the beach and in spite of the presence of three magistrates could not be deterred from their object until the crew of the reserve cutter fired at them.*' (3).

Their object would have been to secure any or everything of use or value that they could lay their hands on. This was the usual form of 'wrecking' as practised in Cornwall. The locals, and those from further inland, looked upon it as their right, even a God given one. Cornwall is not a county of great timber resources, nor one of affluence, therefore the very fabric of a ship together with ropes, tackle and its cargo were irresistible prizes.

> *The* 'Good Samaritan' *came ashore*
> *To feed the hungry and cloathe the poor,*
> *Barrels of beef and bales of linen,*
> *No poor man shall want a shillin.*

runs a verse about a ship wrecked in Cornwall in 1846. (4). There is little evidence that ships were deliberately lured onto rocks by false lights but at times over-exuberance turned to violence. Accounts vary too on the treatment of the survivors of wrecks. Stories range from gallant rescue and compassion, to inhumanity and the stealing of clothes from the unfortunates' backs. All in all 'wrecking' came with poverty and the need to supplement a meagre existence. However legal it was not!

In 1869 the RNLI established a lifeboat station at Portloe. Much discussion had taken place as to where on the Roseland it should be sited with strong rivalry coming from Portscatho, a few miles to the west.

A correspondent to The Royal Cornwall Gazette showed his indignation on hearing that '*it was determined by Captain Ward RN to place the Gorfenkle Life Boat at that most inconvenient place (Portloe) instead of in the south of the bay at Portscatho.*' (5). His challenge was based on access and ease of launch. However, '*to counter them the Vicar of Veryan called a meeting including twenty fishermen of Portloe to consider which was the best place. Naturally enough, the fishermen, by a unanimous vote, declared themselves in favour of Portloe Cove, and pointed out the shortage of men to crew a Portscatho boat.*' (6).

A Liverpool businessman, Joseph Gorfenkle, whose name – with a slight spelling change – appears on two of Portloe's cottages, founded the boat through a legacy. A thirty-three foot, ten oared lifeboat was procured for the station, being brought by train to Grampound Road and then by road to Portloe where Peter Johns was to be Coxswain.

At first the lifeboat was housed at the top of the steep road leading to the cove in the building that was later enlarged to become a church. But to prepare the boat for launching proved problematical. At one quarterly practice the carriage braking failed and the launch crew were unable to prevent it from crashing into a small shop opposite. The inappropriately sited boathouse was then replaced in 1877 by another on the beach. But in 1887, after just eighteen years, Portloe ceased to be a lifeboat station, the vessel never having been called out to a casualty. The boathouse on the beach was later converted into a school, and later still to become the Village Institute. It is now a part of The Lugger Hotel.

In April 1875 the sailing ship *Marie Elizabeth* was driven onto the rocks off Portloe Point during a gale. Loaded with fertilizer she was on passage from Topsham in Devon to Portloe. The ship was a total wreck.

March 1891 saw a great blizzard come to Cornwall. In an ENE gale and driving snow two large ships came ashore near Portloe. The 566 ton iron-screw schooner-rigged steamer the *Dundella*, ten days from the Azores with oranges and pineapples for London, had used so much bunker coal steaming up from Ushant against the gale that she became light and difficult to manage. Attempting to make Falmouth she found herself driven ashore at the Straythe, one mile west of Portloe. Captain Reid saw coastguard's flares telling him that his situation had been noted, and that help was on its way. As a consequence he ordered all to remain on board. '*Several of the crew, over anxious for their safety, defied orders, and Charlie Taylor, the young messroom boy, was lowered over the the side. Suddenly he shrieked, "Haul me up!" but the rope went slack and they saw him standing on the rocks, having slipped out of the bowline. As he tried to get ashore a breaker swirled around the* Dundella's *bows and swept him away.*' (7).

Realising how close to shore they were, Captain Reid ordered the crew to abandon ship. Crewman Kirsten needed assistance having burnt his hands when he thrust the wrong end of a distress rocket into the galley stove! The summoned Portscatho rocket crew took four hours to reach the scene having a dreadful ordeal marching with four horses through deep snow. By the time that they arrived the survivors of the *Dundella* wreck were being warmed in front of the fires of Portloe's cottages.

Much of the fruit was eagerly collected and put to good use, but according to many the cargo also brought with it a small fly with a painful bite to become known as the *Dundella* fly. Much of the vessel was later to be salvaged she being so close to the shore. The ship's bell hangs in Portloe Church while a porthole can be seen at The Ship Inn.

In the same gale the 900 ton *Carl Hirschberg* – Cardiff bound from Hamburg – also drove ashore near Portscatho. A month later it was successfully refloated after a channel had been dug through rock to deep water.

On the 27th September 1897 the Portloe Coastguards heard distress sirens coming from the direction of the Dodman. In response they launched their cutter, the Portloe lifeboat having already been decommissioned, to investigate. The casualties were found to be two Royal Navy warships.

The destroyer HMS *Thrasher*, a four-funnelled thirty knotter, had left St.Ives Bay at 3.00 am with two other destroyers – HMS *Lynx* and HMS *Sunfish* – on a stokers' training cruise (8). They soon encountered fog while off the Land's End and by 11.30 am found themselves directly under the massive cliff of the Dodman having missed Falmouth altogether. Luckily for the *Sunfish* the cliffs were spotted in time and she was able to put about. But the other two struck. With the *Lynx* suffering less damage she was able to kedge herself clear, but for the *Thrasher* tragedy was to befall some of the crew.

On impact the *Thrasher* was severely damaged fracturing a main steam pipe which forced clouds of scalding steam into the boiler room. Three men died but the heroic efforts of Stoker Edward Lynch in managing to drag out injured Stoker Paul were to be recognised. Both men were badly burnt and Paul was later to die of his injuries. For his gallantry Lynch received the Albert Medal from Queen Victoria.

In attendance at the Dodman that day were the RN tug *Trusty*, the destroyers *Ferret* and *Spider* with the Falmouth tug *Triton* being the first to arrive. The *Thrasher* was refloated at high tide and was brought, decks awash, into Falmouth's Carrick Roads.

In October 1898 a mighty 7,000 ton liner *The Mohegan* grounded on the Manacles with a loss of 106 lives. It was reported that Portloe, amongst other places, went mad in anticipation. Would any of the wreckage come their way? A barrel of brandy was picked up by two men at Portholland and handed to the Coastguard. "You must be alone if you want to do a roguery." (9) was the reason for the unexpected honesty. Two men, close friends or not, would probably not be able to keep such a find secret, especially if under the influence of the find's contents!

On the 13th May 1908 a fishing tragedy occurred which devastated the whole community. James Albert Blamey, aged 48, together with young William John Parker, aged 22 and affectionately known as Willie, were hauling pots in their open boat. Returning with sail up they were seen a half-mile east of Portloe to disappear in a severe squall. The empty boat was later found with mast and sail missing near that spot. Some six weeks later Willie Parker's body was found floating some distance off Porthallow, near St.Keverne. The body of James Blamey was never found. Willie's coffin was brought by steamer from Porthallow to Percuil and then on to Portloe where it rested in the Coastguard Boathouse. A funeral and burial followed at Veryan which was very well attended with many tributes paid to a very popular young man.

Portloe's most notable wreck occurred on 2nd February 1914. *The Hera*, a German barque of 1,994 tons, 91 days out of Pisagua, Chile, with a cargo of nitrates was nearing The Lizard in a WSW gale. To Captain Lorenz her

The German barque *Hera* later to be wrecked on The Gull Rock on the 1st of February 1914

position was in doubt, he having to rely on dead-reckoning for three days or more. His hoped for sighting of either The Lizard or St Anthony lighthouses proved fruitless. The Second Mate Petersen reported land ahead and despite the Captain's order for the *Hera* to put about she struck the Outer Stones of the Gull Rock. With distress rockets fired and a lifeboat manned the *Hera* settled fast. The lifeboat capsized and Captain Lorenz and three crewmen disappeared into the night sea. The others from the lifeboat, including the helmsman Alfred Johannsen, scrambled back on deck. An attempt was made to free the other lifeboat, but to no avail. Chief Officer Muhliessen, now in command, led the surviving crew up the masts away from the rising water. On such a bitter winter's night, in a howling gale, the odds were stacked against their surviving till dawn. Cold and exhaustion claimed Second Mate Petersen who passed his whistle up to Johannsen before slipping into the sea. News of the wreck was passed through the Coastguards to Falmouth. (10) The lifeboat Bob Newbon, under Coxswain Hingston, was on her way towed through the heavy seas by the Falmouth tug Perran, accompanied by the tugs Victor and Triton. The Falmouth Packet reported '*in twenty-five minutes of the first firing of the signal the Falmouth lifeboat Bob Newbon was on her errand of mercy.*'(11). Such a practice of being towed was commonplace where the early lifeboats lacked speed, relying upon oars or sail.

After two wet and freezing hours up the masts Johannsen, Third Mate Hoffman, Able Seamen Larsen and Cauci, and Cadet Bersier were rescued thanks to their whistling being heard on board the lifeboat. Nineteen lives were lost including that of Captain Lorenz whose body was washed up at Portloe. All were buried in Veryan Churchyard. The remains of the *Hera* were sold by auction to Harris Bros. of Falmouth for £205. (12) Enough still remains to attract frequent visits from divers.

Thirty-one people were lost in July 1966 off the Dodman with the sinking of the pleasure boat *Darlwin.* Returning to Mylor, off Falmouth's Carrick Roads, with a party that had been to Fowey to see the vessels of the '66 Tall Ships' Race, they encountered heavy seas. It was thought that the ageing *Darlwin* was unsuited to the voyage.

In recent years much publicity resulted from the demise of pop-star Simon Le Bon. Competing with a full crew in the Fastnet Race of August 1985 the yacht *Drum* was forced to take a course close to the shore to avoid huge seas whipped up by a summer storm. Near the Gull Rock she capsized having lost her keel, leaving the entire crew trapped below. A helicopter from RNAS Culdrose was scrambled and the crew were, one by one, led to safety by a Royal Navy diver and winched aboard. Because of Simon Le Bon's high standing in the world of pop music the incident was more than adequately covered by the Press. Speculation arose as to the cause of the keel loss. One theory was that *Drum* had struck Lath Rock, close to the surface at low tide, one mile south of Portloe. Another that she may have clipped the Outer Stones of the Gull Rock. But the most likely cause was that the keel fixings had worked loose. Much amusement followed over the next few days as a small boat from Mevagissey had secured a line to the upturned hull. Owing to the huge drag from the mast and rigging the salvaging craft was insufficiently powered to cope with the tow. On the flowing tide she attempted to reach Mevagissey and on the ebb turned west for Falmouth. Eventually she had to relinquish the tow to a larger vessel which successfully took Drum to Falmouth.

(1) C Noall & G Farr, *Wreck & Rescue Round the Cornish Coast III*, Bradford Barton 1965
(2) *Royal Cornwall Gazette* 11th December 1830
(3) C North, *The Parish of Veryan*, Veryan Parochial Church Council, 1996
(4) J G Rule, *Albion's Fatal Tree*, Pantheon, 1975
(5) *Royal Cornwall Gazette* 11th December, 1869
(6) C Noall & G Farr
(7) C Carter, *The Blizzard of '91*, David & Charles, 1971
(8) R Larn & C Carter, *Cornish Shipwrecks vol 1*, David & Charles, 1969
(9) K C Phillipps, ed. *The Cornish Journal of Charles Lee*, Tabb House, 1995
(10) R Larn & C Carter
(11) S Bird, *Mayday!* Ex Libris Press, 1991
(12) R Larn & C Carter

SUPPLEMENT
THE WRECK OF *THE HERA*

The 19 German sailors that perished were:

Captain J Lorenz

1st Officer L Muhleissen

2nd Officer	W. Petersen	aged 24
Cook	F. Wegner	43
Carpenter	F. Fischer	21
Sailmaker	K. Hammer	30
Donkeyman	A. Marcinek	26
H. Dieber		26
H. Ahrens		
K. Huse		27
P. Illner		21
I. Witt		18
F. Sohderman		
H. Muller		21
R. Laske		
E. Mayer		
W. Smith		
H. Bahr		16
C. Claussen		16

On the stone of the mass grave in Veryan Churchyard, dedicated by the owners Rhederei Aktien Gessell Schaft of Hamburg are these words:

The fog hid the light of the harbour
With danger unseen on the lee
The crew brave and true did their duty
In the face of a terrible sea.

Missing the light sailing homeward
The "Hera" went down in the deep,
Missing their faces we mourn them,
Sacred the spot where they sleep.

All honour to brave brothers resting
Safe home in God's harbour at last.
God's blessing abide with the mothers
Till sorrow and partings are past.

SUPPLEMENT
THE PORTLOE ANTHEM

This hymn was so regularly sung in Portloe that it became known as *The Portloe Anthem*. The sea was at the heart of the whole community.

Brightly beams our Father's mercy
From his lighthouse evermore;
But to us He gives the keeping
Of the lights along the shore.

Let the lower lights be burning!
Send a beam across the wave!
Some poor fainting, struggling seaman
You may rescue, you may save.

Dark the night of sin has settled;
Loud the angry billows roar;
Eager eyes are watching, longing,
For the lights along the shore.

Trim your feeble lamp, my brother:
Some poor seaman, tempest-tossed,
Trying now to make the harbour,
In the darkness, may be lost.

'Gov'ment' in the early 1900's. On the left is The Trap House and Fugler's Close. The main terrace is the Coastguard Cottages with Trevanion, the residence of the Chief Officer, The Boathouse with its slip, and to the right of the Chapel the formerly named Dunstone Terrace

SMUGGLING
THE FAIR TRADERS

The lot of the Cornish fisherman, and indeed the tin miner, was one of hard work in difficult conditions for little financial return. In such conditions to indulge in 'fair trade' was a natural development to raise a living standard from what could only be described as poverty. Smuggling was not for the mere love of adventure or a desire to get one over on the revenue authorities. Like 'wrecking', smuggling helped provide an income of money or kind, and with conscience clear these men were 'fair traders' above any man-made law.

"It is impossible," declared Lord Holland in a speech before the House of Lords, 9th July 1805, *"totally to prevent smuggling. All that the legislature can do is to compromise with a crime which, whatever laws may be made to constitute it a high offence, the mind of man can never conceive as at all equalling in turpitude those acts which are breaches of clear moral virtues."* (1). His thoughts were somewhat echoed by Adam Smith in his definition of a smuggler as *"a person who, though no doubt highly blamable for violating the laws of his country, is frequently incapable of violating those of natural justice and who would have been in every respect an excellent citizen had not the laws of his country made that a crime which Nature never meant it to be so."* (2).

Perhaps as Cornishmen we have painted a picture from a one-eyed viewpoint. So we must not ignore the fact that smuggling did have its dark side. With Dr. Johnson's definition of a smuggler as *"A wretch who, in defiance of justice and the laws, imports or exports goods either contraband or without payment of the customs,"* in mind, violence often accompanied the 'trade'. The smuggler had an obvious enemy in the Excisemen and Coastguards. Fearing not only the loss of valuable trade on capture, the punishment for smuggling was fierce. Often the big time smuggler would be armed, sometimes with an arsenal considerably more powerful than side-arms! The contraband having been distributed inland would be fiercely defended by ruthless men. More than one Customs' Officer had been killed while going about his duty.

Whereas 'wrecking' provided material directly of use to the poor, smuggling on the other hand supplied the whole community from pauper to publican, and from parson to squire. The necessity of sharing 'trade' made a link between all parties. The owner of the vessel had to evade the Revenue cutters while at sea, and dispose of the contraband before arriving at his own port. Signals were arranged between him and the local fisherman. The smaller coves, like Portloe, were ideal for this purpose, and when wind and tide suited there would be a rendezvous between the vessel and a smaller boat off-shore, a transfer of the contraband would take place then the trading vessel would make for her true destination. Once ashore the goods had to be hidden, usually in the homes of obliging persons, possibly farmers, or even the local squire. At all times there being played a cat and mouse game with authority. (3).

Portloe was ideally suited to smuggling activity. In the early nineteenth century the burial register for Veryan Parish provides information of several accidental deaths. In 1803 two young men died attempting to rescue brandy kegs on a Sunday - the very day doubling the 'crime'!

Later in 1823 five brandy kegs were observed near the cove, these being a part of a cargo previously sunk by smugglers, having now broken loose. Local men and boys crowded the beach only to see three kegs smash on the rocks and the other two staved in by the waiting Coastguards. But not all was lost, sufficient brandy was recovered to provide the bystanders with a good drink. In fact one of the fishermen, John Harris, drunk so much spirit that he died! (4).

An old gentleman tells of his father, apprenticed to a shoemaker at the age of fourteen, in his village nearby. The hours were long and holidays infrequent. With a colleague, '*to vary the monotony of work they often turned out for a night's poaching, also going to Gorran or Portloe to fetch home smuggled goods, chiefly brandy. This latter was carried in small kegs, slung by a rope over the shoulders. On one occasion, when returning, they espied at some distance a party of excisemen, and were forced to take to hiding in a field of standing corn, where they remained all day beneath a hot sun, with nothing to eat or drink. On arriving home, the liquor was poured into a wash tray and coloured the right shade with burnt sugar, after which it was returned to the kegs and sold to trusty customers.*' (5).

The Government's fight back at smuggling in the locality came to a head in June 1824 with the Commissions of Customs inviting tenders for '*the erection of a watch and boathouse, slip and channel at Portloe, within the limits of the Port of Falmouth.*' (6). By the following year the buildings were complete. Accommodation then had to be found for the men and their families. The Watch House, or Government House, was the residence of the Chief Officer, his wife and family, and their domestic servants. The Chief Boatman, who had responsibility for the cutter itself, would be allocated the Boathouse. The ordinary boatmen and patrolmen needed to be in cottages in the immediate area. The small terrace of cottages to the seaward of the former Chapel – The Wheelhouse, Anchor Cottage and Caddy Daw – was originally called Dunstone Terrace and was built in the 1820's for this purpose. They were the early 'Coastguard Cottages' along with possibly Bristol House and Cliff House, which in those days was a row of three called Dorsetshire – probably named from the Coastguard's county of origin.

In August 1843, off Portloe, a fisherman's hooks became entangled with a sunken store of 84 tubs of spirits. These were recovered by the Coastguards and were deposited at the Falmouth Coastguard House. Much of the contents had become affected by sea water making it virtually undrinkable. Such an unpalatable mixture was known as 'stinkibus'. (7).

In the community the role of the Coastguard was a difficult one. A review indicated that the recovery rates of contraband or salvage were less than good because of casual relationships between the Customs' Officers, Coastguards and boatmen. It was as easy for a Coastguard to pick up information about a possible landing as it was for a smuggler to learn of an intended raid. (8).

Harris wrote of the practice of manning the stations, avoiding the employment of local persons. '*England's watchfulness and strength is writ large upon the coastguard station, and the men are uniformly intelligent and good-mannered. A strange mixture of blood, Great Britain in epitome, may be found in one small station we halted at, namely, two Irish, one Scotch, one Novocastrian, and one Devonian, not a dash of Cornish blood at a Cornish station. A native might wink the other eye if his own flesh and blood did a bit of free trading in spirits and tobacco, and only run with his "two left legs" after a culprit related to himself.*' (9).

Discipline was tightened with coastguards expected to live with their families in rows set apart from the populace. To discourage them from fraternising with the locals they were given large gardens to encourage self-sufficiency, and keep them out of the village shops. The Coastguard Cottages we know today were built in 1859-60. The land belonged to the Mount Edgecumbe Estate and on the 29th September 1859 land and building leases were granted to the brothers Pentecost, James and William Dunstone. William was a well established carpenter and builder who had constructed many of Portloe's houses, and would go on to build the original lifeboat house in 1869 and the second in 1877. James was a fisherman and coal merchant, Pentecost a shopkeeper working with his mother, who was also a draper. They could be considered as fairly well-off at that time. William would oversee the construction of the entire row of cottages and outbuildings using local labour. When the terrace was complete William took the leasehold of number 7, James number 8 and Pentecost number 9. The Mount Edgecumbe Estate retained the freehold while The Coastguard Service of The Admiralty paid the rental. In 1880 Mr. Elijah Theophilus Langdon, a farmer of Treviskey, acquired the leasehold of Coastguard Terrace and with an agreement of 2nd January 1902 let the cottages to the Admiralty for a set period of 35 years at £105 per annum. The building of the Coastguard Terrace was a very big undertaking for that time and until recently it was always known as 'The Buildings'.

In 1898 Charles Lee in his journal wrote of the Coastguard Cottages' gardens having *'a plague of caterpillars infesting the place. Having reduced the cabbages to forlorn wrecks, they are invading the Coastguard Station in force, and a naval demonstration is projected against them.'* (10). Lee had also had a chat with the Coastguard Chief Officer whom he described as 'an admirable man, universally liked and respected. He has made Portloe the soberest and best conducted station on the coast.' (11).

Serious smuggling had already become a much less frequent activity but as Lee had been told in 1898, *'when the fishing fleet is out in the Channel there is always a Dutch couper about, with a supply of baccy and liquor. The French boats will always give a supply of weak brandy to those who ask, or will fill a bottle with better stuff for a few pence. It is fun to hear their pallyvoozing* (parlez-vousing)' (12).

A Dutch couper or cooper was virtually a floating shop where uncustomed goods were bought for very low prices. Because transactions took place on the high seas no law was infringed, that is, until the goods were brought ashore!

By the 1920's the need for a large coastguard presence in Portloe was diminishing and The Admiralty relinquished their agreement on the houses. In January 1928 Mount Edgecumbe Estate sold the freehold to a Mrs. Emily Dunstone, a hotelier from Gulval near Penzance – possibly a descendant of the original builders? The nine cottages and surrounds went for £700 and now became available for the local people to rent. Various owners held the cottages until they were eventually disposed of one by one as they became vacant. Many coastguards stayed in Portloe, or returned after their retirement. The last to be employed as a coastguard in Portloe, and to retire here, was a Mr. Goddard who lived at Treviskey Hill until the early 1960's.

(1) A K Hamilton Jenkin, *Cornish Seafarers,* Dent 1932
(2) A K Hamilton Jenkin
(3) D du Maurier, *Vanishing Cornwall,* Penguin 1972
(4) C Noall *Smuggling in Cornwall,* Bradford Barton 1971
(5) A K Hamilton Jenkin
(6) *Royal Cornwall Gazette* 23rd July 1824
(7) *Penzance Gazette* 23rd August 1843
(8) D Mudd, *The Smugglers' Ways,* Bossiney 1991
(9) J Henry Harris, *Cornish Saints & Sinners,* The Bodley Head, 1906
(10) K C Phillipps, ed. *The Cornish Journal of Charles Lee.* Tabb House 1995
(11) K C Phillipps
(12) K C Phillipps

The Cornish Twins
Willie and Nancy Johns. Both reached the age of 100 and to the delight of photographers were happy to pose for the camera

The Blamey family of Sunny Corner in 1887. Back row: Herbert, Florie, Adolphus, Annie, Augustine; Middle row: Charlie, William, Lillie, Robina, Dora; front row: Monty, Beatrice and Janie

PORTLOE'S POPULATION
TRADES & OCCUPATIONS

The Census returns taken on the night of 30th March 1851 gives us a snapshot of Portloe in the middle of the nineteenth century. In 1841 the Census showed 312 people living in 74 houses, but by 1851 that number had grown to 89 houses with a population of 364. Four houses were uninhabited and one was being built. Apart from fishing, and to a lesser extent farming, other trades and occupations were needed to support the slowly increasing population. Coastguards and their families, for example, number nearly 60 people. Fishing occupies the waking hours of 38 men and their families. The familiar surnames of Dunstone, Johns, Trudgeon and Blamey account for over three-quarters of them. Other families trying to compete for a share of the fish are: Caddy, Dawe, Frost, Harris, Profit and Williams. Agricultural labouring gives employment to 14 men, while farmers in Portloe itself are Charles Dyer (16 acres), Amos Gay (9 acres), and James Blamey (6 acres).

Fishermen, farmers and labourers, as well as the entire population of men, women and children always needed boots and shoes which suffered terribly from the rough roads and especially from sea-water! The day of the rubber boot had not yet arrived. As a result, Portloe had two 'Master Cordwainers' or shoemakers – cordwain was a kind of leather originally from Cordova, in Spain – Stephen Blamey and James Benallack. In the same trade were Richard Frost and John Trevarton and they are described as 'Cordwainer Journeymen' meaning that they were qualified employees. Within the next generation the term 'cordwainer' disappears in favour of shoemaker.

Making the working-man's clothes as well as his Sunday best were master tailors Richard Blamey and James Dunstow. They employed three tailor-apprentices – Joseph Profit, John Jenkins and John Trudgeon. The women-folk were well taken care of with milliner Elenor Morse making and selling hats. Two young ladies, both called Elizabeth Dunstone, were dressmakers. The Coastguard families usually had a dressmaker among their numbers and Margaret Thomas, daughter of the Chief Boatman, was one, as was her sister Sarah who was a dress and bonnet maker.

The village carpenters are Thomas Blamey and William Dunstone. No-one lists mason or master-builder as their occupation in 1851 but William Dunstone, then 38 years old, would later tender for and build the Lifeboat House and in a later census of 1891 is described as a master-builder.

Margaret Dunstone, the mother of William, is a shopkeeper, grocer and draper at the grand age of 75. She is helped in the shop by her daughter Selina. There is much competition in the grocery business as Mary Bell runs a grocery shop but is only 74 years old! Grace Wiliams is also a grocer.

The New Inn is occupied by Luke Williams, wife Mary and children Luke and Mary. He lists maltster, fisherman and innkeeper as his occupations. Maltster suggests that beer was brewed on the premises, probably in the cellar that is now The Lugger Hotel kitchen. The Ship Inn sees Nicholas Dyer as innkeeper with his wife Mary and six year old daughter also called Mary.

Other essential tradesmen were James Dunstone who was a coal dealer as well as a fisherman. Joseph Dunstone was a cooper, Richard Williams was a basket-maker who would have made fish baskets, or mauns out of willow, and Charles Rundle who was a tinker.

Very few young men in their late teens or early twenties are listed, they are away serving in the Royal Navy. However four young men are 'sailors' and two are 'seamen'. Two describe themselves as 'mariners' – Luke Williams and the wonderfully named Asia Morse.

The Coastguard Station has nine 'Boatmen of the Coastguard Service' together with their families. Government House (Trevanion) is occupied by Lieutenant Joseph Baker, RN, in charge of the Coastguard. A widower, he is living there with his six children, sister-in-law and two servants.

Sixty children are 'scholars' with fifteen being 'taught at home'. Thirty-six children are under five years old. It is recorded that Portloe had two School-mistresses, Harriet Blamey and Grace Williams. Only seven women earn a living from being domestic servants in the larger houses. A visitor to Portloe was the aptly named John Chapple, a Bible Christian Minister who was probably here for a wedding as the word 'marrying' is inserted in the occupation column. Of the elderly population fourteen are listed as paupers, seven as annuitants, three Greenwich Pensioners, one Chelsea Pensioner and one Coastguard Pensioner.

No butchers or bakers appear in the 1851 Census. With fish being the staple meat diet it is likely that rabbit and the occasional home-killed pig supplemented this need. Bread would have been baked at home in the traditional 'cloam' ovens along with cakes and pasties.

In the Government Census of 1891 fishing is the main source of employment with 53 men so described. Farms are the other large employer with 3 farmers living in Portloe itself with another 12 in the nearby areas of Camels, Trewartha and Treviskey, all within walking distance. These employ another 20 people as either agricultural labourers or farm labourers. Younger people under the age of 18 are described as farm servants. 12 women are employed as general domestic servants. Other occupations include masons/ master-builders, carpenters, grocers, drapers, shoemakers, butcher, coal merchant and carriers. There are 2 public houses and a post-office. There is also a cooper, a fish salesman, a boat-builder and a bus proprietor.

Children number 153 with 111 being of school age. Children as young as 3 are listed as scholars. Children up to 8 would be attending the newly

A pony and chaise with Mr. Molvey, Granfer Tom Trudgeon, Mrs. Molvey and daughter Rose. Notice the scales outside May Johns' shop

opened Portloe School where the new Schoolmistress Miss A Belle Lintell from Reading was employed. Miss Lintell, aged 36, was lodging with John Frost, a farm labourer, and his wife Mackenzie in their house near the Coastguard Station. Harriet Blamey, 74, is also described as a schoolmistress, she lived next to The Ship Inn.

Three weeks before the census was taken 'The Great Blizzard' of 9th March 1891 had driven the Dundella ashore near Portloe. Eight men were boarding with families in the village; 3 ship and boiler cutters, 2 ship cutters, 2 iron cutters and a supervisor of ship breakers. They were all from the Plymouth area. There can be little doubt that they were here to salvage what thcy could of the wreck. They would have brought some welcome income to Portloe.

The fishermen are once again predominantly of the families Trudgeon, Dunstone, Johns and Blamey. They account for 14, 12, 9 and 6 respectively. Other fishermen include Richard Caddy and Robert Dawe who are remembered by the name given to the large rock below The Boathouse. Obviously the rock had a name before Caddy and Dawe were fishing and was possibly called 'Carrek Dowr' meaning 'Freshwater Rock' in Cornish. One of Portloe's two streams tumbles down the rocks along side it. Also listed are WT and WJ Banfield, John Gribble (mentioned in Charles Lee's Journal), Richard Lean, John Martin, Samuel Profit and William Trevarton.

Three farmers living in Portloe are Robert Dunstone (farmer and corn merchant), James Cocks (farmer and carrier), and Thomas Dunstone. At Camels two farms are run by Henry Trounce and William Symons. Matthew Langdon Blamey is an agricultural seed merchant near by. At Cruggan Susan Trounce is a farmer, as is Catherine Gray at Trenisson. Treviskey has 2 farmers, Joseph Blamey and ET Langdon. Trethennal Farm, overlooking Portloe, sees Thomas Blamey, yeoman, while at Trewartha Hall the farmer is William Nicholls.

At Sunny Corner William Guy Blamey and his sons Adolphus, Herbert and Augustine are the village carpenters. Herbert and Augustine are apprentices. Montague, although only 8 at the time, would also join the profession. They covered all kinds of carpentry work, but coffins provided reliable and regular work. They also took on the task of 'laying out' and putting the bodies in the boxes ready for burial. William and his wife Robina Jane had 5 sons and 4 daughters living with them in 1891.

The Census lists one boat-builder, Arthur Johns, whose wife Caroline is a shopkeeper with her sister Thomasine a dressmaker. Other dressmakers are Evaline Trevarton and Liza Dunstone with Emily Hodge and Lily Williams working from the Coastguard Station. Samuel Blamey runs a grocery and Fanny Blamey Johns combines a drapery with a grocery store. Francis Dunstone and son, and William Rundle are shoemakers.

Unusual perhaps is the female village butcher Hannah Maria Blamey, a larger than life character who, it was said, could carry a bullock on her back with ease! In the late 1800's she lodged at Edgecumbe House with Edward Williams and his wife, but was soon able to take over the freehold in 1907 for £165. She conducted her business from the cottage, doing her own slaughtering and butchering in buildings and a yard 50 paces up the hill. These are now converted into garages. She bought her livestock from farms at Treviskey, probably much from Alfie Julyan, and would drive the bullocks down the hill to her slaughterhouse. Hannah did not marry!

In 1891 the Sub-Postmaster is Richard B Johns combining his job with that of being a fisherman. Benjamin Dunstone is a carrier and James Cocks lists carrier as an occupation alongside farmer. Edmund Dungey runs The Ship Inn, living there with his wife Emma and children Carlendra 8 and Charles 6. Charles was killed during The First World War while serving in the Royal Navy. His name appears on the Veryan War Memorial. Occupying The New Inn is landlady Nancy Dunstone, her daughter Eliza is servant/cook. Her other two children are Louisa 13 and Maurice 8.

Portloe had 3 masons or master-builders, William Dunstone 78, who had erected the lifeboat house, now the Church, in 1869 for the sum of £159. Samuel Fugler 41, who lived at Fugler's Close and whose family would have built the house, and Franklin Davis of Puckey Hill. His son Joseph 14 was a mason's apprentice as was his other son Frederick aged 12. Matthew Dunn of Sunny Corner was a cooper who would have made barrels primarily for fish. John B Dunstone was a fish salesman who probably sold the catches of his two fishermen sons John and Thomas, as well as those of the other fishermen.

The Census of 1891 also lists the Coastguards and their families living here at the time. The Coastguard Station (Coastguard Cottages) has 52 residents. Five Coastguards are listed with their wives and children. They are not of course local people but have come from different parts of the country. Being employees of HM Coastguard they went where they were needed and only spent a few years at each station. The Census reflects this showing the birthplace of each child. Only the very young were born in Portloe, the others at various stations along the south coast from Dorset to the Isles of Scilly.

Tom Blamey, born in or around 1874, was the son of Matthew Langdon Blamey, an agricultural seed merchant of Camels. An astute businessman he accumulated wealth as an auctioneer and valuer as well as investing in the fast growing hotel trade. The prestigious Nare Hotel was opened by him in partnership with four other local investors. He was able to have the impressive cliff-perched Broom Parc built in the early 1900's using local bricks made from the mud from the banks of the Fal at Trelonk near Ruan Lanihorne. He employed many staff including William Rawling as chauffeur and gamekeeper, and Jimmy Morse as head gardener. His eccentricities included a morbid fear of being and catching cold. He was said to often wear two coats and hats and to have his boots warmed before putting them on. The seats of his motor car too had to be so prepared. Tom Blamey had a locked bag for his mail deliveries. Only he and the Postmistress held a key! A keen field-sportsman, he had extensive shooting rights in the area, and with his love of all sport he left £3,000 in his will for the establishment of a Veryan sports and social club. Further money was left towards the construction of a sea wall at Portloe, although it was not until 1959 that the 'pier' was completed.

Veryan Parish has natural limestone occurring especially at Gwendra near The Nare Hotel. This high grade stone was burnt in lime kilns in the area to provide lime for mortar, whitewash and for fertilizer. Portloe had a kiln near what is now the Church, the arched remains of which are clearly visible today. Look carefully at the high wall of The Ship Inn car park and you can just see part of an arch of another kiln. According to a notice of sale of 1792 Portloe had a timber-yard, a coal-cellar and a lime kiln, all in the charge of Pentecost Williams, the tenant of John Daw. In 1814 The Ship Inn was

Hannah Blamey – the village butcher. It was said that she could carry a bullock on her back!

leased with buildings converted into and leased as lime kilns. It is probable that later, limestone would have been imported from the Plymouth area. In 1841 a tragic accident occurred which the local newspaper headlined '*Another Child Burnt*' *The West Briton* of 16th July reported '*a little girl about five years old, daughter of Mr. Paine of the Coast Guard, Portloe was unfortunately burnt to death by attempting to take a roasted potatoe (sic) from the lime kiln.*' It is likely that lime-burning in Portloe ceased soon after this date, no such occupation is listed in the Census of 1851.

In pre-Second World War Portloe May Johns sold 'pop' in alley-bottles. These Codd's bottles contained a marble (alley) valve system. At a cost of two pence (2d) one penny was returnable as a deposit, but many bottles got broken deliberately just to obtain the marble!

In the 1950's Portloe was still a thriving community with two shops. At Cliff Gardens Auntie Edie sold groceries and confectionery. The shop's entrance door is now gone but the cobbles on the road outside show its position. An old fashioned balance scales sat on the counter with row upon row of bottled boiled sweets at the back to tempt the children. The shop sold everyday items from light bulbs to aspirins, and from Corona to tea - coffee was yet to become popular! A large shop-window was added in the mid 60's and the entrance moved to the former lime kiln.

The other shop was at Cob Cottage, the large bay being the shop window. You went up steps and through a door long since gone. Like Auntie Edie's shop, the goods for sale were much the same and with no competition on prices being then controlled by the 'Resale Price Maintenance' regulations. Run by Luke Johns in the 50's it was then taken over by Peter Woods.

The Post Office was run by Fred and Ivy Trudgeon who also sold stationery, post-cards and ice cream. The public telephone box was then situated on what is now the entrance steps. Fred and Ivy ran the P.O. from 1920 to 1964. Before 1920 the Post Office, grocery and drapery occupied a position on the corner of Godolphin House, now part of The Lugger Hotel. Fred and Ivy both died in 1964. Their daughter Doreen and son-in-law Jack Trudgeon, who retired from fishing, took over, and were there for 26 years.

Fred Johns still milked cows in the village as well as keeping poultry. His wife Linda made clotted cream in a shed in their garden at Bristol House As a young child living in Proncha Cottage I (KJ) would feed the chickens with stale bread – eating some myself! Fred also ran the garage/petrol station situated at the entrance to what is now the car park.

Early evening sunlight, shadows, smoke and seagulls – serenity!
Looking towards the Church from the Gow

Local Place-names & Their Origins

Finding the origin of a place-name is fraught with problems. Even experts, ancient and modern, often disagree or even give up with certain examples. Over many years place-names change both in pronunciation and in spelling; sometimes owing to 'up country' mapmakers' spelling assumptions and sometimes because of the slow development of writing within the general populace. Cornish language origins tended to become Anglicized with the slow but sure decline in Cornish speaking. The place-names around Portloe may have origins that have become misted with time so the reader is advised to bear in mind these two words, "probably" and "possibly".

Bessy Beneath: from the Cornish C. bos bennath. – Home of the blessed, the site of an early sisterhood.

Broom Parc: C. Field or enclosure with broom.

Calendra: C. Farmstead with holly trees.

Camels: C. cam hals – crooked or winding cliffs.

Carne: C. a rocky outcrop, but in this case almost certainly refers to Carne Beacon, a grass-covered barrow.

Cruggan: C. possibly caer oghan – camp with oxen, or more likely crug – a burial ground.

Dodman: C. ?maen – stone or rock. Dodman in 1560, Deadman in 1700. O Padel in 1988 suggests Dudman after a family that farmed Bodrugan in 1469. The Dodman appears to have been called Penare at an earlier date. (compare Nare Head)

Elerky: C. swan pool or stream.

Gwendra: C. white sand.

The Jacka: C. It has been suggested chogha or choca – the chough?

Kiberick: C. keber – beam of wood, place of wood? Even driftwood?

Melinsey: C. melyn – corn mill.

Nare Head: C. Pennare (Penare) – high headland. Penare Point in 1540. Pennare wollas – lower Pennare, Pennare wartha – higher Pennare.

Pendower: C. head at the stream's end.

Portholland: C. Porth henlann – cove of the old churchyard (probably predating St.Michael, Caerhays) Portalan in 1290, Porthallan in 1380.

Portloe: C. Porth logh – inlet pool, Porthlowe in 1653, Portlow in 1690.

Tregenna: C. Farm at the mouth of a gulley.

Tregony: C. goon – downland, settlement of the down? Trigoni in 1201 – may be farm of Regni? Tregny in 1540. Note: Tregony pronounced "tregny" not as would be expected in Cornwall "TREEgoany", indicates that its name is a contraction of its original form. Compare Tregonhay.

Treviskey: C. Farmstead below a wood.

Trewartha: C. Upper farm or settlement. Even higher town.

Veryan: from the Parish Saint, St Symphorium (1281) to Severian (1525) to St Veryan.

THE DODMAN, THE NARE HEAD & THE GULL ROCK

The finest promontory on the South Cornish Coast, 368 feet above the sea, The Dodman presents a natural eastern boundary to the Portloe fishermen's home grounds. Over the centuries the headland has appeared on maps as Dudman, Dodman and especially in the nineteenth as The Deadman – a name which is still used by the local fishermen. To add to the confusion, Murray in the tourist handbook of 1859 calls it, '*The Deadman pronounced Dodman.*'(1). The origin of the word is certainly from the Cornish Language with 'man' a corruption of 'maen' meaning rock or stone. The meaning of 'dead' or 'dod' is conjectural.

J Henry Harris writing a hundred years ago summed up the charm of the Dodman. '*The highest headland in the county is one of those places of solitude where depression will not stay. Hour after hour one may pass on the bluff headland without seeing a human soul or hearing a human voice, and yet feel one's spirits elated in the silence. With a mere half-turn of the head one can see the whole Cornish coast, from The Lizard to the Rame, and beyond, and all the ocean traffic passing up and down. Then below, a sheer fall of four hundred feet, are the little crabbing boats, mere specks upon the blue, shoaling into green and breaking into foam upon the dark, weathered rocks. And then the wind, blow which way it will, must sweep this headland, bringing with it the scents of heather and wild flower untainted, as though in all the world there was no such thing as smoke, and factories, and areas of pollution.*' (2).

To the west of Portloe, beyond The Gull Rock, lies the magnificent Nare Head, 260 feet above sea-level with Veryan Bay stretching to The Dodman in the east and Gerrans Bay to the west. Originally named Pennare – the high headland – the name got shortened to Nare through the common practice in the locality of dropping the first syllable of a place-name. For example Trewartha is often Wartha, and Treviskey – Viskey.

A late nineteenth century guide cared more for the weary walker in its dismissive statement, '*Nare Head is a bold headland, but scarcely of sufficient individuality to tempt the possibly tired pedestrian out to its extremity.*' (3). Why do we doubt the writer ever having been there? Its setting is superb and the views from both sides are magnificent. In clear visibility even the towering Eddystone lighthouse can clearly be seen! And what better than to look down onto The Gull Rock on a summer's evening.

During the Second World War Nare Head became *'a film set with special effects by Ealing Film Studios. The whole purpose was deception. From the air at night it became a railway system, with lights to simulate signals and the partly shaded illumination of a railway station.'* (4) With Nare Head a safe distance to the east of Falmouth Docks, and correspondingly Nare Point to the west of Gillan on the Helford, decoy systems were set up. Communications were the objects of air attacks and the rail link with the Docks was vital. So if bombers dropped their loads over either of these two headlands then Falmouth would be spared. When the flight-paths of approaching aircraft were ascertained one of the two decoy stations would be activated. Lights would be switched on powered by generators controlled from bomb-proof shelters. Elaborate plans were made to simulate the effects of bombing the 'Docks' including oil-baths which could be ignited as well as fast burning piles of wood and explosive devices. Later during the 'Cold War' the Nare was to have underground listening posts, still there, and occasionally open to the public. This beautiful headland with its panoramic views, once the property of the Caerhays Estate, is home to peregrines and a rich variety of wildlife.

The Gull Rock, 125 feet high and 6 cables (400 yards) eastward of Nare Head has had a history of name changes. In Leland's time in the sixteenth century it was known as The Gray, and yet in a seventeenth century *Coasting Pylot* it is called The Gull Rock. With the name Gray or Grays still used by fishermen up to a few years ago, what a shame that such a distinctive title should have alternated with a name that is given to well over a dozen similar rocks around the Cornish coast.

The Rock is a valuable reserve for seabirds. In 1967 eight burrows were found which could have belonged to puffins, but only one bird was seen in the sea about half a mile away. Ornithologist and historian, Roger Penhallurick found puffin eggs there in 1951, while later in 1968 conversing with a Portloe fisherman was told that a few puffins were there up to about ten years previously, while remembering large flocks of 'sea parrots' about the Rock in the 1920's. (5). Although the puffin no longer nests anywhere along the South Cornwall coast, its cousins in the auk family, the guillemot and the razorbill still flourish, together with cormorants, shags and many types of gull, especially the kittiwake.

In former times of a more meagre existence The Gull Rock was a source of seabirds and eggs for food. '*To offset the lack of other food, seabirds of many kinds were formerly consumed. Amongst these were sea-larks (?), seapies (oyster catchers?), puffins, shags and even gulls.*' (6). Carew, writing in 1602 said of these seabirds, '*all of which content not the stomacke with a like savourinesse, some being good to be eaten while they are young, but nothing toothsome as they grow elder.*' (7).

To the south-west of the main rock lie the Middle and Outer Stones. These too have an alternative name being referred to by The Admiralty in a pilot of 1947 (8) and by Lake in 1867 (9) as The Whelps.

Once owned by the Manors of Elerky and Trewarthenick the Gull Rock was given to the National Trust in 1989 by Michael Trinick, its former Regional Director in Cornwall, to mark his term of office as High Sheriff.

H.M.S. Cornwall salutes the handing over of The Gull Rock to the National Trust in 1989

(1) Murray, *Handbook for Travellers in Devon & Cornwall*, Murray 1859
(2) J Henry Harris, *Cornish Saints & Sinners*, The Bodley Head 1906
(3) Ward & Baddeley, *Thorough Guide S. Devon & S. Cornwall*, Dulau 1885
(4) Acton & Carter, *Operation Cornwall 1940-44*, Landfall Pub. 1994
(5) R. Penhallurick, *Birds of the Cornish Coast*, Bradford Barton 1969
(6) A. K Hamilton Jenkin, *Cornish Homes & Customs*, Dent 1934
(7) R. Carew, *Survey of Cornwall*, 1602
(8) *The Channel Pilot (Part 1)* Hydrographic Dept., The Admiralty 1947
(9) *Lake's Parochial History of Cornwall*, Lake 1867

The 'Town' showing the Church, the enlarged and improved former Lifeboat House, the lime kilns and to the right one of the village shops. Notice the donkey and chaise in the corner!

Miss Ellery's Private School 1927. Back row: Jack Trounce, Betty Elliott, Audrey Elliot, Irene Bennett, Flora Tripp, Miss Ellery; middle row: Ethel Tripp, Mary Bennett, Alice Dustow, Dorothy Parker; front row: John Bennett, Ursula Whitcombe, ? Whitcombe and Gracie Trounce

Worship & Education

With the Parish Church being at Veryan and with other non-conformist chapels being scattered throughout the area provisions were made for Portloe to have its own place of worship. A Bible Christian Chapel was licensed at Portloe in 1837. An early tiny Chapel was in use on the land adjacent to Beach Hill. By 1843 the congregation was meeting in a large building with a gallery and even chandeliers. But just a few years later, in July 1857, during a summer storm, it was struck by lightning. The blast caused serious damage with several of the congregation being injured and indeed one small boy was killed. (1). At the time *The Royal Cornwall Gazette* reported, '*The Chapel bears marks of a violent attack. Much of the roof is shattered, several pews torn, and many of the footstools crushed. Clogs were burnt on the feet of the females and others had their shoes and stockings destroyed. A captain of a vessel was burnt on his leg, and a youth was carried from his seat a considerable distance as the lightning made its escape.*'

By 1882 a new chapel was built on the same site and continued to be well supported. Sundays were not only days of rest and worship but times for dressing in one's finest. In 1898 Lee's *Journal* informs us that '*most of the men wear soft black wideawakes (soft felt hats with low crowns and wide brims) and a neckerchief. The younger men wear bowlers and clean white collars.*' (2).

Round about this time the temperance movement had become popular with The Band of Hope vociferous in the Parish. But not all of Portloe's population gave them their support. Lee tells us that '*the last time Naylie got drunk was when The Band of Hope came here. He always got drunk then on principle, to show he isn't one of them!*' (3).

Sam Rickard remembers pre-war Sundays in Portloe, with a 'Grand Parade' on Whit Sunday to the Chapel. The women wore new dresses and hats, the men smart suits. On the following afternoon Portloe's children had a half-day off school with tea in the Sunday School followed by Sports in the field. At Christmas at Sunday School each child received a book. The teachers included Peter Johns (Granfer Peter), Uncle Luke Johns, Uncle Johnny Trudgeon and

Jane Johns – all putting a lot of their time into the Sunday School. In the 50's and 60's the teachers included Jack Trudgeon, Joe Blamey and Albert Blamey.

Eventually the Church and Chapel congregations became too small and a merger was made in May 1992 with Portloe's Mission Church. This All Saints' Church was formed in 1896 in an altered and enlarged former lifeboat house. After one hundred years as a church it was extensively refurbished so as to function for joint services as well as a community centre. The Chapel was offered for sale and has now been converted into a dwelling. The Church bell is from the freighter Dundella, wrecked near Portloe in 1891.

In 1891 a school was opened in the cove in the building that was the second lifeboat house. The Mistress was a Miss Lintell, aged 36 and originally from Reading. Children up to the age of eight received their education there, those that were older had to take the long walk to Veryan. Attendance was never good, often averaging only thirty or forty per cent, and with an attendance of only seventeen in 1910 the future looked bleak. The school subsequently closed in 1915, the building later becoming a village institute.

During the 1920's a private school catering for some dozen or so pupils was run at Sunnybank by a Miss Ellery. Former pupil Alice Baker, then Alice Dustow, tells us that she would walk the three miles from her parents' farm at Trempissick, near Tippett's. She would leave home at 7.45 am to reach school by 9.00, returning home after lunch with homework for the afternoon. Fees were 6d per week with 1d extra for sums! Apart from these two schools, Veryan, Portloe's larger neighbour had the school that educated Portloe's children.

(1) C. North, *The Parish of Veryan*, Veryan Parochial Church Council, 1996
(2) K. C. Phillipps, ed. *The Cornish Journal of Charles Lee*, Tabb House 1995
(3) K. C. Phillipps

Inns, Hotels & B&B

Nineteenth century Portloe could boast of two public houses – The Ship Inn and The New Inn. The latter dates from at least 1821 when John Williams was landlord, his family were still there running the business in 1851. A guide of 1885 informs us that '*The New Inn lets a sitting-room and bedroom, and though small, is accustomed to cater for visitors.*' (1). In 1887, according to the Veryan Parish Rate Book, The New Inn was owned by a Mrs. Roberts and occupied by James Dunstone who, as reported in *The Royal Cornwall Gazette* was fined in January 1870 for '*keeping late hours*', and again in March for '*refusing to admit the Police.*' *The West Briton* of 7th June 1877 advertised The New Inn to let as '*old established but newly repaired – apply to Moyle's Chacewater Brewery.*'

The reign of the Dunstone family in the running of The New Inn is complex and confusing. Census returns show that in 1881, 61 year old widower James Dunstone is combining the job of publican with that of a farmer of 6 acres. Living there with him are three very young illegitimate grandchildren – Eliza, Louisa and Herbert, together with married couple Edward and Sarah Blamey. Meanwhile, elsewhere in Portloe lives 62 year old widow Ann Dunstone who is described as a retired innkeeper, coincidently also looking after two young grandchildren – Walter and Annie. Just ten years later in April 1891 the inn was run by a 38 year old widow Nancy Dunstone, who lived there with her 3 children and lodger Joseph Williams. Much must have happened in those ten years!

A well told story refers to Landlord James Dunstone, probably the one already mentioned, who was known as 'Black Dunstone' and was believed to have been hanged for smuggling! Unfortunately we are unable to substantiate this popular "myth" but why let the truth spoil a good story?

In 1891 the need to augment trade by diversification was apparent when *The West Briton* of 21st May had the inn to let, '*also doing good grocery and baking business.*' But perhaps the writing was on the wall for the public house when by August 1891 an ejectment notice was served on Mrs. Dunstone and her licence refused. Some years later on 15th July 1909 the *Gazette* advertised

The Ship Inn in the 1930's. The man is Edward Francis '*Muggy*' Dunstone. *Muggy* was a fish jouster - a hawker of fresh fish

to be sold '*a block of houses at Portloe with cellar, boat-building shed, etc., known as the* '*Old Public House*'.' The following month the lot was sold for £69. (2). The site of the "old" New Inn was almost certainly that which is now occupied by The Lugger Hotel.

The Ship Inn was certainly in existence in 1814 and probably well before that. In 1821 John Gay was landlord, and in 1851 Nicholas Dyer ran the pub. His widow Catherine was still there as landlady some thirty years later. *The West Briton* of 7th September 1893 reported that landlord Edmund Dungey was fined for selling adulterated brandy – a crime repeated in June

1900 by landlord Mr. Cocks, possibly the James Cocks who according to the Census of 1891 was a farmer in Portloe. *The Gazette* of 3rd October 1907 reports that James Cocks was assaulted by a customer '*who he stopped singing!*' (3). By then the Ship had been enlarged, following a fire, and improved from the former two-roomed, cob-walled predecessor which was known in the village as 'the drinking kitchen'. (4). With the growing holiday trade in mind Mrs. Winifred Cook, in 1939, advertised '*bed and breakfast, board residence and every convenience.*' (5).

The Ship enjoyed good trade in the 1960's and 70's where the hosts, Dudley and Eileen Johns, welcomed locals and holidaymakers alike. This was the era of the great British seaside holiday when cheap packages to Spain had hardly started and the Government of the day had imposed a maximum £50 that could be taken on holidays abroad. The area around Portloe had two caravan and camping sites, Cecil Blamey's field at Carne catered for visitors as well as the many families from the Truro and St.Austell areas. Situated just one field away from the wonderful Carne and Pendower beaches on many occasions it would overflow into adjoining meadows. With another smaller campsite at Tregenna, the two provided an excellent source of customers wishing to eat and drink at The Ship Inn or at Dudley's brother-in-law, Charlie Cracknell's pub – The New Inn at Veryan.

Born at Treviskey, Dudley's long reign of over twenty-five years was due partly to the wonderful family support he received and also to his endearing ability to make all people welcome wherever they came from, be it local, holidaymaker or foreign traveller. He had a talent to appraise instantly a customer so as to be able to share a joke, a story or treat the serious minded with polite service. In conversation with local Henry Johns one summer evening he invited two newly arrived visitors to join them. "Where are you two from, Cap'n?" inquired Dudley politely. "Oh I am from Birmingham and my friend is from Coventry," came the reply. With straight face and a matter-of -fact tone Dudley countered with, "Henry's from Caragloose and I'm from Viskey." The two visitors accepted this information with a somewhat puzzled countenance! As an example of how much he was loved and appreciated can be seen from the fact that most of his regular customers would say, "I am going down to see Dudley," rather than, "I am going to the Ship." Dudley Johns was The Ship!

The Ship in the 1950's – the little cottage adjoining was still not incorporated into the pub

The Inn continues to serve locals and visitors alike and no doubt will always be the provider of excellent Portloe crab dishes. The interior is crammed with an extensive and comprehensive photographic record of Portloe.

One summer's day in 1948 Charles and Lillian Powell were driving along the coast from their home in Gorran Haven when they happened to arrive in Portloe. While looking around the harbour they saw a property for sale. Then called 'Tregarrick' – home on the rocks – it certainly lived up to its name. It was directly on the water's edge and dominated the tiny cove. It was in very poor condition with no electricity, mains water or sewerage. Included in the sale, behind Tregarrick was a row of derelict fishermen's cottages, three storeys high with fish cellars below. It is believed that the cottages were deliberately made uninhabitable by the owners, Major and Mrs. Jack, to avoid housing evacuees during the War. The authorities had commandeered the cottages but were unable to make use of them because the roofs had been stoved in. But despite all this Charles and Lillian Powell could see the site's potential.

At that time the Powells were Stewards at the Cornish Riviera Club at Carlyon Bay but yearned for their own hospitality business. In the Autumn of 1948 they decided to throw caution to the wind and purchase the still available Tregarrick and its cottages. The Jacks had used it as a tea shop with associated bakery products – a follow on from its days as The New Inn where baking was carried out over fifty years earlier. During renovations a large 'cloam' oven (one made of pottery) far too big for one family, was found.

After two years of hard work the renovations were complete. Charles and Lillian Powell opened for business in March 1950. They decided to call their new venture 'The Lugger Hotel' after the many Cornish luggers – small two or three masted ships with lug-sails – that had called at Portloe over the years bringing essential supplies. The old row of cottages was demolished to form a car park.

Beach Hill and Tregarrick between the Wars, the site which was to become The Lugger Hotel.

A Guide of the early 50's sees the Powells advertising with an eye to the 'out of season' break with *"Situated in the beautiful Roseland District, is one of the warmest places in the country, ideal for winter and summer holidays. Every comfort considered. Personal supervision Mr. and Mrs. Charles Powell."* (6).

In 1956 the business was expanded by taking a lease on Godolphin House. Previously let as appartments, the windows were still taped up against bomb blasts from the War. Upstairs was turned into extra letting bedrooms, while downstairs a craft shop was established.

1970 brought further expansion with the purchase of the freehold of Godolphin House and the adjoining fish cellars which after major refurbishment were brought into Godolphin House. This brought the number of rooms to twenty. The former School and Institute was purchased and converted into a staff residence. By this time the next generation of the Powell family, Colin and his wife Hilda, had joined the business, later to be followed by their children Stephen and Julie.

In addition to the public houses, in 1935 Mrs.Shea was offering Bed & Breakfast at Cliff House. In a hiker's guide of 1932 the author describes '*the proprietress of Cliff Cottage, a most kind hearted lady, will be only too glad to assist or advise the rambler.*' (7).

In 1960 Mrs.Joyce Rounsevell of Camills Farm at Camels offered, '*4 double, sitting room, bathroom, B&B 10/6 to 12/6 per night, children from 8/6, on a bus route, with pretty gardens, overlooking the sea.*' (8).

(1) Ward & Baddeley, *Thorough Guide to S. Devon & S. Cornwall,* Dulau 1885
(2) H. L. Douch Unpublished ms. *In preparation of Old Cornish Inns* 1966
(3) H. L. Douch
(4) C.F.W.I. *The Cornwall Village Book,* Countryside Books 1991
(5) Kelly, *Directory of Cornwall* 1939
(6) *The Blue Book Guide to Cornwall,* Liddicoat, Newquay, c1952
(7) V. Thursby, *Fourteen Hikes Along the Cornish Coast,* Rankin Bros. 1932
(8) D. Murdoch, *Farm Holiday Guide* 1960

Transport & Communication

Until the second half of the nineteenth century Portloe's transport by road was very limited or even non-existent. The inhabitants of the village were virtually self-sufficient and did not want or need to travel far. The majority, apart from those in seagoing careers, not venturing outside Cornwall in their entire lifetimes. In those days travelling across land in horse-drawn carts or donkey and chaise was slow and hazardous. Cart tracks that wound their way out of Portloe to the surrounding villages were narrow and poorly maintained. The sea provided the main means of transport and communication. People, if they wished, could travel to nearby coastal villages by boat.

Towards the end of the nineteenth century roads began to improve. In 1894 Rural District Councils took over the responsibility for roads and road maintenance providing materials and labour. With the better standard of roads, public transport could now provide a reasonably comfortable, although very slow, journey to other villages and the two market towns of Truro and St Austell. As early as 1873 *Kelly's Directory of Cornwall* informs us that Banallack and Blamey are carriers hauling goods to and from Portloe to Truro on Wednesdays and Saturdays, and to St Austell on Fridays.

The early buses were of course horse-drawn. In the 1891 Census William Trevarton of Portloe had his occupation listed as a 'bus proprietor'. He too would have provided a service to Truro and St.Austell on market days. Normally two horses pulled these covered carrier's carts with the journey taking up to four hours, including stops, each way! Starting from Portloe in the early morning and getting back at around 8.00 pm was quite normal. To avoid the stresses and strains of the horses passengers were expected to get out and walk up the hills – a practice that we shall later see not only applied to horse transport! This early form of bus continued right up to the 1920's when visitor Folliot-Stokes in his writings tells us that while enjoying a conversation with some old Portloe fishermen he heard a girl call out, "The bus, the bus!" Approaching us down the village street was an antiquated vehicle, drawn by a most antiquated steed. The vehicle was packed with

Pre-Great War Portloe with a merchant ship waiting to ground to be unloaded

villagers, all in their Sunday best. They were wedged in between a miscellaneous collection of merchandise. On the front seat sat an old man with a large sewing machine. At his side a girl holding at arm's length a fashionable hat. Each of the inside passengers clasped some bulky purchase. "Where do they come from?" we asked an old salt. "Truro," he wheezed. "She be the Truro bus. She do belong to go twice a week to Truro and once to St.Austell." This wagonette was at that time the only means of transport to town.' (1). To refresh the horses pools were maintained at the tops of each hill, at Treviskey and at Camels.

After the First World War the earliest examples of motorised public transport started to appear in Portloe. In 1921 Albert Morse, along with his son Gerald, established the coaching business 'Roseland Motors'. At about the same time Ernie Tregunna started a bus service from Penvose, near Portholland. The demand for public transport was now increasing as the service became more comfortable and much quicker.

Before long the 'Pride of Veryan', a petrol-driven bus with solid tyres and spoked wheels, became a familiar sight around Portloe and Veryan. It was one of the earliest type of motorised public transport in Cornwall. Now the time taken to reach the market towns was reduced to an hour or so, a tremendous improvement. Public road transport had really taken off. The

Pride of Veryan was designed to carry around twelve passengers, but it regularly had many more on board, with goods carried on the roof. Rosalie Hawkridge in her book 'Veryan Remembered', informs us that 'it had two wooden benches running from front to back, so that the passengers sat facing each other. The fare to Truro on Wednesdays and Saturdays was 2/6 and to St.Austell on a Friday 3/-' (2).

Early engines struggled with the heavy loads and when facing a hill the younger men were told to get out and push! Drivers could be heard shouting "Whip behind! Whip behind!" when auxiliary man-power was needed! In those days the new road through Trewarthenick had not been constructed, so buses had to climb the steep hairpin at Dabb's Hill just on from Tregony Bridge.

Two 'milk-rounders' bring in supplies. The building on the left was the second Lifeboat house, then the school

The Pride of Veryan in the 1920's. The first motorised public transport in the area and one of the first in Cornwall

When not carrying passengers these early buses would double as carriers. With the seats removed anything could be transported, and often was. Bags of coal, bales of hay, animal hides, fish - anything that needed moving. Sometimes, so overladen, they would need a local farmer with his tractor to pull them up the hills! When the job was completed, a quick wash out, the seats put back, and the bus was ready for fare-paying passengers again.

Between Albert and Gerald Morse, and Ernie Tregunna a regular and reliable service to Truro and St Austell was established. A weekly bus on a Thursday went to Percuil to link with the steamer to Falmouth. After the closure of the Percuil facility the service transferred to meet the St Mawes ferry. Early bus services to St Austell would go via Portholland. Overloaded with passengers they would drive along the Bal, the narrow cliff road between West and East Portholland. Later this practice was stopped by the local authorities as it was considered too dangerous. On Mondays the Pride of Veryan was available for private engagements. Sundays would rarely see a service excepting a bus to Carne Beach on a sunny Sunday afternoon during the summer.

During the 30's and 40's newer Commer buses came into service, continuing through the War years when headlamps were so dimmed that it became dangerous to drive after dark. In the late 30's the Morses ran excursions to London. The fare was 10/-. The bus travelled up on a Friday, returning on Sunday with a stay at The Great Western Hotel. After the War the 1950's saw the peak of bus travel at Portloe. Very few people had a car, and buses provided a means of getting to work as more found employment in the shops and offices of Truro. The 'Workers' Bus', which left Portloe at 8.00 am and returned at about 6.30 pm was regularly full. Shopping in Truro became popular and in those days the bus parked with its door left open so that shopping could be placed on the seats and returned to later. In addition it was possible to entrust your shopping list to the driver who, in your absence, would shop for you! Laundry for The Lugger was taken to and brought back from Truro by bus. Parking by Portloe's Church, the laundry baskets would be slid down the hill to the hotel. Another unusual service provided by the Morse's was to take, on Mondays and Wednesdays, hot pasties from the mothers of Portloe's children to Veryan School, this in the days before school dinners were introduced.

Albert and Gerald Morse's bus climbs the hill past the Ship Inn in the late 1920's

A late bus on Saturday nights enabled young people to visit the cinemas in Truro. Returning at 11.00 pm it was always full, often over-full. During the 50's the buses were 29 seater Bella Vistas, and the later Bella Vegas could carry 33. Former buses and coaches of the Royal Blue fleet, coloured blue and cream, were resprayed in the red and cream of Roseland Motors, Ernie Tregunna's buses had a chocolate and cream livery. Sometimes these buses were so overcrowded, especially on Saturday evenings that many people would be standing in the aisles. Approaching Truro many of the passengers would get out and walk into town past the Police Station in Tregolls Road. This would prevent the driver being charged with overloading! On the return journey the same procedure would take place.

Roseland Motors also ran shopping trips to Plymouth as well as the popular Bank Holiday Mystery Trips. Not knowing where the destination would be added to the excitement for children and adults alike. While at secondary school in Truro, I (MR) remember that it was always Roseland Motors that took us to sporting fixtures, not just in Cornwall but to Plymouth and Exeter too. One annual fixture from Truro School which Roseland Motors undertook was to Canterbury in Kent, an excursion of three or four days duration! Daily school runs became important especially with the opening of the Secondary Modern in Tregony.

By the end of the 1960's passenger numbers were dwindling as more people owned cars, and in 1970 Roseland Motors diversified successfully into the motorcar trade, eventually moving to larger premises at Tresillian. The original garage, just beyond Treviskey, was demolished and a house built on the site. Ernie Tregunna retired from the coaching business at the end of the 50's going to work for Jimmy Harris at his garage at Bessy Beneath.

Sea transport was used for the import of heavy materials. 'Flat iron colliers' frequently unloaded supplies of fuel directly onto the beach. These vessels were able to ground safely between tides to be unloaded. Other shipping included the many 'milk rounders', little sailing coasters that fetched and carried over relatively short distances. Their cargoes included animal feeding stuffs, timber, fertilizer and limestone for the kilns. All the goods were taken away by horse and cart or mule carriers. Road communications were blocked by snow and ice in the hard winter of 1947. The Portloe

Fred Johns' garage and shop in the 1960's with a Roseland Motors bus. At the back is Fred's cowshed

fishermen used their boats to bring back bread and essential supplies from Mevagissey.

In 1893, according to Kelly's Directory of Cornwall, Richard Blamey Johns was the Sub-Postmaster, combining this job with that of fisherman. Letters were received through the nearest railway station at Grampound Road, via Ruan High Lanes, arriving in Portloe at 10.30 am. Mail was dispatched at 1.55 pm weekdays only. Peculiarly Portloe P.O. could issue postal-orders but was not authorised to pay out on them! In 1926 the Post Office was being run by Frederick Trudgeon.

A public telephone was allocated to Portloe in 1923 and before long was followed by private lines.

(1) A. G. Folliot-Stokes, *The Cornish Coast & Moors*, Stanley Paul, 1928
(2) R. Hawkridge, *Veryan Remembered 1860 – 1926*, Roseland, 1986

The cobbler's shop of William Rundle (*Penticost*) is the small building in the centre

---

The seat on the Jacka. Left to right Jackie Trudgeon *(Tiddle Jack)*, Wallace Lean, William Arthur Blamey, Richard Dunstone *(Dicky Boy)*, ? , Fred Trudgeon, Edward Frances Dunstone *(Muggy)* and Bob Dawe.

THE STORIES & JOURNAL OF CHARLES LEE

We have already encountered Charles Lee's observations of Portloe from his journal written in 1898. He was writing short stories from 1890 to 1914 and chose Portloe to be the setting for a collection of tales, written around 1910 under the title of *Our Little Town*. Though not Cornish, he was considered to have been one of the best ever 'outsiders' to understand the Cornish. Historian A L Rowse felt that he caught the dialect and speech mannerisms better than any other writer – including Cornish ones! Sir Arthur Quiller-Couch hailed '*a writer who could use our (Cornish) speech as we natives use it, understand our ways genially; who – perhaps above all justified himself as an artist.*'

Simon Parker in his *Chasing Tales (The Lost Stories of Charles Lee)* writes, '*Lee was fishing for true Cornish voices during his stay at Portloe, the setting for his masterpiece* Our Little Town, *a series of wickedly funny and accurately observed vignettes of local life. His characters are so believable that it seems certain they were all based on real inhabitants.*' (1). One of the main characters is Penticost, '*a curmudgeonly*' soul who runs the cobbler's shop. – the chief meeting place of the male population in the village of Porthjulyan (Portloe). Fred Johns, who lived in Portloe and died shortly before his one-hundredth birthday, was born in 1898 – the same year that Charles Lee stayed there. Fred remembers a one-legged shoemaker called William Rundle whose shop was virtually the men's institute for relaxation, smoking and lively debate.

The position and description of Mr. Rundle's shop fits that of Lee's Penticost's. Both William and Penticost were Bible quoting Methodists frequently using Chapter and Verse to combat any situation. In Penticost's shop Lee describes a prominent notice that in all probability really did hang in Rundle's shop.

NO SWEARING NOR DAMMING
NO RELIGEON EXCEPT PENTICOSTS, HE CAN T HELP IT.
NO WIMEN ALOWD
NO MORE THAN FIVE TO SMOKE AT ONCE
NO TAKING WAX-ENDS WITHOUT PERMISSIAN

Lee in *Our Little Town* comments, '*I would ask you to admire the subtle distinction implied in the first of them. The second in order to prevent unseemly wrangles in a place that holds fervent Wesleyans, ardent Churchmen, and fiery Bryanites. The saving clause is a concession to our hosts weakness for garnishing his conversation with obscure and terrible texts from the minor prophets. The third calls for no comment whatsoever. The fourth is a needful sanitary regulation, having regard to the exiguous dimensions of our quarters. Without the protection of the fifth, Penticost would soon be a ruined man, with wax-ends twopence a piece, and their superior fitness for binding fish-hooks and splicing knife-handles generally recognised.*' (2).

The Cobbler's Shop was a one-storied building in the main street. You entered by going down steps to below ground level. Its small window was set just above the level of the street. It is now Joey Trudgeon's bathroom!

Charles Lee in his *Journal* reported that, '*William the shoemaker has a hard time of it in the winter. As many as four and twenty able-bodied fishermen frequent his shop which is no bigger than a hat box. Sometimes the chaff and practical jokes are more than he can bear; he weeps and declares he'll give up the shop. When he gets teased, he picks up his hammer which he flourishes and invites one and all to show their pluck by letting him hit their hands. "That's the only answer William have got" was the explanation. The shop is described as being littered with scraps of leather, a broken window, patched never cleaned "yet he knows everybody that passes, and though living in his underground den, he is the man to get information from. No minutest feather of gossip flies up the street without blowing into his door." The door by the way, and the step or so within, are dignified by the name of 'the lobby'.*' (3).

Now long out of print, to read *Our Little Town*, best obtained in the compendium volume *Cornish Tales* published by Dent in the 1940's and 50's, is a joy to all who know and love Portloe. Just like the names of the characters, the place-names are changed. But the discerning reader will easily spot Churchtown as Veryan, St Kenna as St Austell, Tregany as Tregony and of course Porthjulyan is Portloe.

There follows three extracts from *Cornish Tales*. One astutely describing the village in the years before The First War, the second of fuchsias and cats, and thirdly an insight into Portloe's relationship with the Coastguards.

'Physically and politically, all Porthjulyan is divided into two parts – the Town proper, and Gov'ment. (The Coastguard Station). Taking the letter U for the groundwork of our survey, I would ask you to impart a slight outward slant to the two main uprights, and to consider them as two steep roads running inland up two narrow valleys. Where the basal curve begins, there begins Porthjulyan on either side, the town to the left, Gov'ment to the right. A low cliff or spur of the hills divides the two parts, so that each is invisible to the other; but follow the road as it humps itself over this cliff, and from the midmost point you can obtain a comprehensive view of the whole place.

First turn seawards. You look down on the cove and its two beaches – the town beach with its serried array of boats, some forty in number, and ranging in size from the little skiffie-boat in which the farm boys and their maidens take their penn'orth of sea on summer evenings, to the big black seine-boats lying high and dry with their stems poking out into the street; and the Gov'ment beach, with its solitary Gov'ment gig afloat at the foot of the Gov'ment slip (The Boathouse) – a spick and span fine lady in blue and white, decorously bobbing and curtsying all day to the indifferent rocks and the disdainful gulls. Wheel about half a turn to the right, and the town is before you, a long narrowish street, curving gently down and away from you to the beach, where it twists sharp about and then straightens itself again for the climb up the valley; with houses set close on their side like partners in a country dance, and other houses scattered here and there on the slopes behind, like the old folks looking on.

Now turn about, and your eyes are dazzled with Gov'ment whitewash; first the whitewashed boathouse with its whitewashed wall about it, then a white-washed fence enclosing the Gov'ment cabbages; above that, , the Chief Officer's whitewashed villa (Trevanion), four-square and vigilant like its master; above that again the men's whitewashed quarters (Coastguard Cottages), crouched under the hilltop in the discreet attitude enjoyed by official dignity and reserve – to wit, with their backs to the road and the town and the common folk thereof. A few cottages stand about in huddled groups, with the awe and influence of Gov'ment upon them; they have a timid air, one fancies, and have whitewashed their faces at least, if not their sides and backs. Over in the town Porthjulyan despises whitewash as a vain and doubtful gloss on honest stone, and is stiff against whitewash, that mark of the Gov'ment beast, and has a text ready on its tongue that is hard upon the whited wall.

At Porthjulyan no household is complete without its fuchsia bush on either side of the door – comely sentinels in green picked out with crimson and purple – and its sleek family of cats curled up on the slab (a Cornish cooking range) beside the stewpot. An event without parallel elsewhere is of daily occurrence at Porthjulyan when the boats come in. As the first keel kisses the sand, cats, white, grey, tabby, and tortoiseshell, appear from all quarters and scamper down to greet their masters. The sight of half a dozen big-booted men stumbling up the beach, each one preceded by a proud cat with heavenward pointing tail, or by an abject cat that casts itself at intervals in paroxysms of grovelling affection before feet that have much ado to keep from treading on it, is not without its tender humour.

As for the fuchsias, their likes for size and multitudinous blossoming are not to be found in all the countryside.

We are down on the beach baiting hooks, drying nets, and so on. Gov'ment having nothing else to whitewash for the time being, is out the cliffs with pails and brushes, whitewashing select portions of the Cornish coast - a stone here, a boulder there, along the coastguards' path. A spar appears on the horizon. Who sees it first? The Gov'ment look-out man, posted on the cliff-top with a big telescope for that purpose and no other. What happens then? A ringing of electric bells, a shouting through telephones, a casting down of pails and brushes, and a general turn out of the entire Gov'ment force. In ten minutes the Gov'ment gig is lying on its oars outside the cove, the chief boatman is on the cliff with flags, pistols, and signal rockets, and every likely point for a mile along the coast has its blue-jacketed watcher. What chance have we of capturing that spar? What can we do but stand by and give vent to our feelings in ironical cheers when the gig returns with its booty in tow?

Now consider the habits and methods of Gov'ment as exemplified in the further history of that spar. It is hauled up into the watch-house. The chief officer approaches it with measuring tape and notebook; he studies from every point of view, he goes home and writes to headquarters, giving its dimensions every way, the number of nails in it, the hour and minute of capture, and copious particulars of the state of the wind, weather and tide. Does the farce end there? I trow not. Something about the spar arouses the stern suspicions of Gov'ment, and for days the chief officer's brow is black with care, and his fingers with ink. At last Gov'ment decides that no treason or felony is discoverable in the spar. "Sell the spar" said Gov'ment. No expense is spared in advertisement, and soon the whole world knows that a proud and powerful Gov'ment has captured a fourteen-foot spar off Porthjulyan, and is ready to part with the same for a consideration. The sale is held, the spar successfully disposed of, and Gov'ment wipes its brow, drops the resultant half-crown into its pocket, and returns to its peaceful whitewashing.

Now you are in a position to understand and justify our attitude towards Gov'ment – an attitude subtly compounded of smouldering irritation and good-humoured contempt. In our eyes Gov'ment is the cosmic villain of the piece, loathed and laughed at by all.'

Lee concludes *Our Little Town* with these words, *"...the stranger within our gates is sacred; of him we keep silence, save from good words. But if you cannot come, the loss (believe me) is yours, and (I assure you) ours too. And so good-bye, and 'wish'e well.'"*

In his *Journal* of 1898 Charles Lee beautifully and astutely observes Portloe's characters and customs. He wrote of what he saw in note form and accurately recorded the local dialect. Firstly Jimmy the Fiddler who followed in his father's footsteps to entertain in a time before radio and television. Jimmy lived alone enjoying amusing the village children with his music. '*They sit as quiet as mice. Ruddy face, white hair and whiskers, upper lip clean shaven.*' Jimmy was begrudgingly offered some charity when the fishermen returned to the cove. '*Someone generally gives him half a hundred pilchards (which he is accused of selling), or a couple of small ray.*' Jimmy also made picture-frames to sell but he had to be very careful so as not to endanger his 'club pension'.

The forename Naylie has often been used in and around Portloe. It is a shortened form of Cornelius which was pronounced Cornaylius and hence Naylie. The following recounted from Naylie's youth could be taken to be of the 1830's or 40's. '*Naylie told me*' noted Lee '*that a farm labourer's wages were seven shillings a week. The daily fare was pilchards and potatoes, on Sundays a slice of fat pork, about four inches square and an inch thick, was baked in the middle of a potato pie. A common article of diet was bannock, an immense flat cake of barley-bread on a hot iron plate. Many's the time Naylie has slipped into the kitchen when his mother's back was turned, torn off the corner of the half-baked bannock, dipped it in the treacle jar, and devoured it. Note the treacle, sugar was too dear; so was tea. A substitute for tea was a crust burnt brown and soaked in hot water.'*

James Johns was a retired fisherman of 78 years who lived in a cottage next to the New Inn, and like many Portloe men was astute and above all, a realist. Lee tells us that James is making a garden, and many have offered plants. But James doesn't set much store by promises. He knows that when some people are asked to do a thing they say, '*"Ess-ess-ess-ess." He doesn't believe in "Ess-ess" people. When a man says, "Well, I'll see what I can do," or "Don't know, but I'll try," then he has confidence in him. The "I'll try" man for him, not the "Ess-ess-ess-ess" man.'*

The old seat on The Jacka was, according to Lee's observations of 1898, an old spar supported on stones. '*This is Uncle Willy's seat, and he sits in the sun, his stick behind him (no handle, he holds it fine-lady fashion) sucking away at his pipe, his tongue ready with a retort or a yarn. Someone gives him a match and bids him be off into the "lew" and light his pipe again. Off he goes and comes back puffing. It seems to me, it is the chief occupation and aim in life of every person and thing in Cornwall. This "getting into the lew".'*

The spar seat on Beach Hill has Ted Trudgeon, Cyril Johns, Ernest Trudgeon, Richard Dunstone (*Dicky Boy*), Arthur Emmett, a visitor?, Gerry Trevarton, Charlie Cracknell and '*Bristol*' Joe Blamey

A translation for those who need it follows this entry in Lee's *Journal* for 15th October. '*A man at Trewartha got drunk and scat up the cloam. So next day his wife gave him a sherdy pasty for crowst.*' (A man at Trewartha got drunk and broke the crockery to bits. So next day his wife gave him a pasty made with the shards of earthenware for his lunch.).

The absence of a designated barber in Portloe was noted. '*Male ablutions*' Lee wrote, '*when of more than a perfunctory kind, are conducted in the front garden. If you want to get shaved and don't care to do it yourself, you stand at your door with razor, towel, basin and soap, etc., until a friendly mortal passes. Him you enlist, and bring a chair into the garden, and sit and submit to his tender mercies. It is not etiquette to offer payment, but if a small boy or girl of the tonsor's begetting is around, you offer the child a penny for sweets.*'

Charles Lee gained inspiration in Portloe in 1898

(1) S. Parker, ed. *Chasing Tales*, Giss' On Books, 2002
(2) C. Lee, *Cornish Tales*, Dent, 1941
(3) K. C. Phillipps, ed. *The Cornish Journal of Charles Lee*, Tabb House, 1995

On 3rd July 1912 a trio of photographers came to Portloe – Hughes, Thomas and Burrow. Two can be seen on the beach setting up their tripods. A row of cottages can be seen in what is now The Lugger car park

The village with The Jacka to the left and The Downs beyond taken from Flagstaff

THE VISITOR
IMPRESSIONS IN PRINT

A few writers of travel books have waxed lyrical when reporting their impressions of Portloe. But for many, Portloe was not on their itinerary and tended to be ignored by or unknown to the early twentieth century traveller. Two late nineteenth century visitors seemed unimpressed with the houses but commented on one aspect of fishing when they wrote, '*Portloe is a little fishing village at the mouth of two narrow converging combes, and is well known for its lobsters. The cove is rock girt, and the Coastguard Station is about the only tidily kept domain.*' (1).

Before the First World War, Harper, covering most of the Cornish coast saw more than the beauty of the village but perceived its failing economy. He wrote, '*Portloe is a gloomy inlet amid dark overhanging cliffs. Down there is the poor fishing village, in a primitive state, absolutely untouched by pleasure seekers, and apparently not thriving in its fishery. But its situation down there below the echoing cliffs reverberating to the mocking cries of the sea gulls, is magnificent!*' (2).

Between the Wars an extensive tour was undertaken by Folliot-Stokes to include not only the Cornish coast but the moors as well. The author was more than impressed with Portloe, and to such an extent that his purple prose at times goes somewhat over the top! '*From Nare Head we reached the steep slope of Jacka Point, and saw beneath us the fishing village of Portloe. Let us drink in the spirit and beauty of a fitting end to a lovely day. We engaged a room at the little Ship Inn. A few dozen cottages, a steep valley, a stream, a small cliff-guarded cove, brilliant colouring and a wondrous surrounding growth of flowers and ferns.*' (3). Later in the day Folliot-Stokes observed the village wagonette – a horse-drawn bus – and remarked that it '*was the only means of communication, bar the post, that Portloe has with the outside world of care, commerce, and catastrophes. Lucky Portloeians!*' (4).

After a night's stay at The Ship Inn the author was even more impressed, and penned '*What a morning followed! In its golden alchemy the little village was a poem, almost a prayer. The smoke from one or two early fires rose like incense. Every gable and boat's mast was crowned with a motionless gull. A cuckoo was calling up the valley, and nearer, several thrushes were singing. The less abrupt sides of the cove were covered with sea-pink and samphire. House martins were skimming over the brilliant green water like snowflakes that had become possessed of a pair of dark blue wings; and the drowsy Atlantic murmured softly as it almost imperceptibly swirled around the rocks. That early morning vision of Portloe was worth going to see.'* (5).

It might be thought that Folliot-Stokes and Harper had used all the superlatives and select adjectives leaving nothing for the later professional visitor. But not so. J. Hockin, with good Cornish insight wrote in 1936, '*Portloe lies under a sort of billowy plateau of plain, wide curving, thickly hedged fields amid a tumble of cracked cliffs, turf-topped and many angled and chasmed by an infinitesimal cove. Sharp grey rocks, clear deep green water, clusters of thick white cottages slipping down hillsides, the chugging of boats and the laughter of gulls – in cramped little Portloe. All these sights, sounds and colours so characteristically Cornish, South Cornish I should say, are heightened and concentrated. Portloe seems absolutely lost for all its Cornishness, and unrelated even to its metropolis Veryan.'* (6).

To the writer of the tourist guide Portloe continued to provide inspiration to the poetic. A guide of the 1950's informs us, '*this delectable Cornish fishing village hides in a small creek of its own. To reach it you descend a lane that narrows and steepens with every hundred yards, between tall hedge-topped banks to emerge unexpectedly, in the true heart of Portloe, the diminutive but ever busy slipway.*

> *Village, even hamlet, seems too grandiose a term. For there is little more than an eyebrow of cottages, stone and slate built, curving round the edge of the creek and rising to the headland beyond. On the other side of the road that skirts their front doors, the springy heather-clad turf drops steeply to the rocks and deep blue water below, intersected by rough stone steps and tracks that only a goat or nimble child can negotiate. Parents can look almost vertically down on their offspring at play on the slopes, diving from the rocks into the clear water; or on the slipway which is, of course, the focal point of the community's interest.*
>
> *Here are a few small boats; here in abundance, barrels of tar, tins of paint, coils of rope, cork floats and nets, lobster pots, rusting anchors, discarded oars, tattered sail-cloth and accumulated junk of all kinds. Here beats the lively*

heart of Portloe. Leaning from the balcony of the small inn that almost literally overhangs the slipway, you may feast your eyes upon the scene, and inhale the composite aroma of seaweed, tar, paraffin, stale fish, lead paint, oilskins and old rope from dawn till dusk Could you ask anything much better of life? It is to be doubted.' (7).

The celebrated Sir John Betjeman felt able to write, in 1964, that Portloe '*is one of the least spoiled and most impressive of Cornish fishing villages.*' (8). We would like to think that even after forty years Portloe can still warrant Betjeman's boast.

Drawn and engraved by William Daniell, R.A. in 1825. Portloe with the licence of an artist!

(1) Ward & Baddeley, *Thorough Guide, S. Devon & S. Cornwall,* Dulau, 1885
(2) Harper, *The Cornish Coast,* 1910
(3) A. G. Folliot-Stokes, *The Cornish Coast & Moors,* Stanley Paul, 1928
(4) A. G. Folliot-Stokes
(5) A. G. Folliot-Stokes
(6) J. R. A. Hockin, *Walking in Cornwall,* Alexander MacLehose, 1936
(7) From a 1950's guide, title unknown
(8) J. Betjeman, *Cornwall, A Shell Guide,* Faber & Faber, 1964

Fishing boats ready for action just before hostilities would enforce most to be laid up

Percy Wheeler, brought to Portloe by the War, would stay, marry and raise a family

Wartime Portloe

Barbara Turner tells us that just after The First World War a disturbance occurred that resulted in the reading of The Riot Act! A group of soldiers arrived in Portloe bent on causing trouble. Frederick Trudgeon was home from hospital for a few days having been badly wounded in September 1918. One of the soldiers pushed him over and in so doing caused the Portloe men to take action. "All Hell broke loose!" she says. A casualty of The Great War was 19 year old John Arthur Johns of Portloe. He was killed in 1915 while serving with The Royal Navy.

In 1939 at the outbreak of World War Two Portloe became a sad and sorrowful place. Most of her young men had been conscripted into the Army and Navy and sent abroad. Fishing virtually ceased with only three boats working throughout the conflict. During the summer of 1940, with the threat of a German invasion, coastal defence measures were put into place all along the Cornish coast. The slipway at Portloe sloped gently back from the beach almost to the Church. Army engineers arrived and constructed tank traps and a barrier wall which ran from the bottom of The Jacka path across the slipway to what is now the entrance to The Lugger Hotel, effectively cutting off the beach. Parts of the wall still remain. Tall concrete pyramids were erected at the top of the beach, one can still be seen, on its side, halfway down on the left. Any boat below the wall had to remain there for the duration of the War! A concrete air-raid shelter was begun on land outside Beach Hill Cottage but was not completed until the end of the War – it was demolished during the 60's.

Early in the War two ships from a convoy were torpedoed off Portloe. Two local boats went out to search for survivors but none was found, just an empty lifeboat. On another occasion a barrage balloon was sighted off the cove, it had probably slipped its moorings at Falmouth. Fishermen went out, brought it in, and tied it to a ring-bolt at the top of the beach. So, just for a few hours, before the authorities arrived to retrieve it, Portloe had its own aerial defence! The West Briton reported a Hurricane's attack on a German Dornier 17 off The Gull Rock in 1940. Just after three in the afternoon

Mr. J. P. Elliott of Trethennal Farm, while in a field above Portloe heard what seemed to be machine-gunning. "I could not see anything," said Mr. Elliott, "but immediately after I saw a plane crashing down about two and a half miles out from Portloe and I saw what I thought to be a member of the crew who had bailed out. The plane struck the water with great force. It went under at once and disappeared. About a minute later the man came down near the same spot." Gordon Trudgeon of Portholland also saw the crash and saw one of the occupants of the plane bail out. One of the Portloe boats went out with Tom and Gilbert Trudgeon, Cyril Johns and a visitor towards the spot where the plane was thought to have gone down but nothing was found in the rough sea.

At Camels, by Broom Parc corner, Army and R.A.F. personnel were encamped in '*Bill*' Rounsevell's field and together with others billeted in the village, worked in The Jacka radar defences above nearby Manare Point. Firstly manned by The Royal Artillery and later by the R.A.F. and the W.R.A.F., the women being put up at The Pendower Hotel. Many service-men fell in love with or fell in love in Portloe. One such person was Percy Wheeler, he was to marry, settle down and raise a family here.

The Canadian crew of an aircraft with engine trouble had to take to their parachutes one evening over wartime Roseland. The first landed near Ruan Highlanes, the second at Melinsey and the third just made land at Camels while the plane crashed into the sea. The lucky airman at Camels had to be extracted from a thorn bush!

A British plane was spotted low over the sea off Portloe by Ivy Trudgeon, who saw it ditch into the water. Fred Trudgeon and another fisherman went out in their boat and brought two pilots ashore where they took great care of them. Sadly both airmen were later to lose their lives in combat.

Portloe and its surrounds provided homes for many evacuees. They mostly arrived in June 1940 from London, Bristol and Plymouth being collected at Truro Station and taken to the British Legion Hall at Veryan. Three teachers accompanied them, together with two billet officers who decided where the children would live. Numbers at Veryan School swelled to 170, with 87 being evacuees living in Portloe, Veryan and its catchment area! In order to cope, the School at first taught the local children for one half of the day and the evacuees for the other. The strain was later to be eased by the use of The British Legion Hall as a classroom.

People in Portloe were kept busy on the land, growing food for the War effort. '*Digging for Victory!*' as the posters exhorted. Every available piece of land was cultivated. The Ministry of Food was paying a £10 per acre subsidy for growing potatoes. Older fishermen skilled in the art of net making were occupied in the construction of camouflage nets, large quantities of suitable string having to be sent up from Porthleven! Others joined the task enabling one massive net to be fabricated every week.

Portloe's wireless sets were powered by accumulators which had to be regularly charged. Gerald Morse of Roseland Motors would collect and deliver these 'wet batteries' so that Portloe could keep up with the news from home and abroad.

As hostilities slowly ceased servicemen began to return home. With mixed emotions and uncertain thoughts for the future, pleased to be back but aware that many would never return, they were welcomed with great enthusiasm. As each Portloe man returned, members of the Band would get the big bass drum out and march through the village with them, collecting cash and singing *"for he's a jolly good fellow"*. Veryan Parish also had a 'welcome home' fund for servicemen and women.

After the War Portloe's fishing fleet once again became active and very soon the numbers were up to twelve.

The Regatta of 11th July 1907 showing the diversity of craft and the Official's steamer

Regatta Day on shore. A time to dress in one's finest

Portloe at Play

Many of Cornwall's south coast fishing villages, including Portloe, held regattas; these being especially popular and prevalent before the First World War. The fierce rivalry that naturally occurred in the fishermen's work was seen in the competitions of sailing and rowing. But this was not the age of strict regulation in building racing craft. Competing with normal working boats would always lead to controversy over hull widths, sail area and age. For one of these reasons, in 1900 the boats of Gorran Haven were thought to have too unfair an advantage. As a result the Portloe and Portscatho men refused to race against them! Despite local differences regatta days were looked forward to as much needed relief from the daily working routines.

One Saturday in 1946 saw Portloe's first sports and carnival since 1938. *The West Briton* reported that '*despite the inclement weather, the festive day, which concluded with the dancing of the Flora through the village, was a great success.*' Mr. J. E. Blamey, Hon. Secretary, told a *West Briton* reporter, *"The whole village has been looking forward to the revival of our festive day. We made up our minds that whatever the weather it should not damp our enthusiasm."* Attractions included sports for both children and adults, sheaf pitching and many sideshows and stalls. Holidaymakers joined in and were also enlisted as judges, The organising officials were: C. Cracknell, J. E. Blamey and F. C. Trudgeon. Some winners of the men's races were E. Gilbert in the 220 yards, B. Kendall in the 440, and R. Kendall in the veterans' event. In the carnival Mary Johns, Ethel Trudgeon and Jill Cracknell won prizes in the children's section. In the humorous category the winners were J. Trudgeon, B. Trudgeon and F. Trevarton.

During the 1950's Festive Day gradually evolved into Harbour Day – centred around the beach and harbour itself. The adult sports events were dropped but children still raced on the beach. Many stalls were set up around the harbour area, while the fishermen ran boat trips to The Gull Rock. Many crowded into the 18 foot craft at a time when insurance cover was scarcely considered! A silver band was in attendance and the afternoon ended with the always popular and much demanded Flora Dance through the streets. To finish the day a dance was held in the Village Institute.

The Silver Jubilee of 1977 saw Portloe stage fun events based around the cove with raft races, swimming and stalls on the beach. Up to fairly recently this Portloe Harbour Day was graced with a visit from the Falmouth Lifeboat and, when available, a helicopter from R.N.A.S. Culdrose. Boat trips to The Gull Rock were once again very popular but by now only registered passenger carrying vessels were used. Over the years much money was raised for charitable purposes, but as with many village events problems arose with insurance cover, the organisers' enthusiasm being tempered by fears of accidents and claims.

Our local newspaper, *The West Briton*, reported The Harbour Day of July 1982. '*Paddles dip furiously as a raft race gets under way at Portloe last week, watched by a crowd of 2.000. The races attracted 22 entries. After a series of heats the cup went to the Portloe Fishermen. The award for the most attractive raft was won by Maneater the entry of Mrs. A. Quinney and Mrs. P. Armstrong. The Ship Inn was runner-up. Lanner Band played and the evening ended with a pig-roast and fireworks display.*'

A Portloe Harbour Day of the late 1980's with a visit from the Falmouth Lifeboat and pole-fighting between the boats of Dave Rounsevell and Chris Mlynski

The Harbour Day of August 1996 took place on a blustery and showery day. Planned boat trips and the R.N.L.I. rescue demonstration had to be cancelled, but a helicopter flypast by the Air Ambulance and a visit by an inshore rescue crew went ahead. '*Portloe based all-female band Maiden Voyage played to a very appreciative audience for 15 minutes before the heavens opened, and continued their program after the ever popular Bash Street Kids entertained with their circus skills.*' was in *The West Briton* report.

For a short period after The Second World War Camels hosted the Veryan Cricket Clubs home matches. Surprisingly the field that was used has at its centre a granite scratching post! A later move to Trewartha saw the Cricket team based on the families of Tregunna, Kendall and Johns. Portloe's children played cricket in the road above the harbour with a fish box for a wicket. If you were caught three times off The Lugger roof you were out! Sam Rickard tells us that, "Sometimes a window would get broken, but there were plenty of places to hide down there. It was like a rabbit warren." He remembers too that pre-War every boy had a hoop as a prized possession.

The Ship Inn Darts Team c1980. Back row: Roy Webster, Peter Moyses, Eileen Johns, Dudley Johns, Clide Tregunna, Graham Trudgeon, front: Philip Webster, Steve Powell, Bill Tregaskis, Colin Clark and Malvin Clark

The Ship Inn has of course been a place of recreation with successful darts teams, and in the 90's a formidable quiz team in which the authors together with John Richards and Ray Bell all enjoyed competing.

Portloe & District Band c1935. Back row: Geoff Morse, Will Trudgeon, Bert Trudgeon, Herb Johnson, Fred Reynolds. Mid row: William Arthur Johns, Cliff Johnson, Charlie Cracknell, Fred Dowrick, Andrew Frost, Peter Blamey, Jack Trudgeon. Front row: Bill Johnson, Sylvanus Johnson, Reg '*Itchy*' Johns, Joe Chenoweth, Benny Johns, Joe Blamey, Hedley Buddle. Sitting: Donald '*Titch*' Reynolds and Albert Morse

In 1929 a Mr. Richards invited all interested men in the village, whether they could play or not, to meet together to form a band. Frauleen Kufel tells us that very soon with the inclusion of bandsmen from Veryan and the surrounding area it became necessary to name it Portloe and District Band. The first bandroom was a loft above the Fishermen's Vats in the centre of the village, long since demolished. Music soon echoed around Portloe on practice nights held twice a week. Their progress was much appreciated and they were soon to be joined by Joe Chenoweth who made an excellent bandmaster. Membership was flourishing with one father and his two sons cycling from Merther and two brothers travelling from Caerhays. After a while the bandroom was considered unsafe necessitating a move to the

Men's Institute on the beach where meetings were held on Tuesday and Friday evenings. On a fine Friday a concert might be performed outside followed by marching around the village to the tune of The Floral Dance attracting a retinue of dancing locals and visitors alike. Confidence was growing encouraging the Band to enter a competitive concert at Redruth. Although not winning, the Band was complimented on their dress and deportment! With a Ladies Committee being formed to help, especially with fund raising, a smart and popular band was ready for engagements at church fetes, sports' days and carnivals. Every Christmas the Band played carols at Portloe before visiting Veryan and the neighbouring hamlets. On Boxing Day it would be the turn of Tregony and Mevagissey. The outbreak of war in 1939 saw a six year period of inactivity with the valuable instruments safely stowed away in the Methodist Chapel. The Band was reformed after the War with new boys together with a girl who had been taught by her father. Unfortunately within a few years numbers began to tail off with other attractions like dance-bands and the early days of television taking their toll. After twenty years The Portloe and District Band had finished.

The Institute was a venue for billiards, later to be replaced by the more popular snooker. In later years Jack Trounce had a snooker room at his home at Trenisson where the team competed in local leagues.

Filming *The Camomile Lawn*. Portloe is wartime Penzance. The breakwater (pier) became the quay. In the boat is Chris Mlynski, Roger Elliott, Terry Hipwood and Bill Spears. On the quay John Richards, Peter Cumming, Peter Lloyd, ? , an actor and Jackie Trevivian

PORTLOE IN FILM & TELEVISION

In 1935 Portloe was busy with the filming of scenes for *Brown on Resolution*, soon to be retitled *Forever England*. John Mills and Jimmy Hanley starred in a war story set in the Mediterranean during 1914. Variety magazine called it '*A milestone in British pictures.*'

Treasure Island was filmed by Disney in 1949 using the Carrick Roads at Falmouth as well as extensively filming around The Gull Rock. This film will be remembered for the delightfully over-the-top performance of *Robert Newton* as the archetypal *Long John Silver*.

The arrival in 1963 of the crew to make the British comedy *Crooks in Cloisters* caused great excitement in the village. The stars were all household names being regularly seen in films and on television. Barbara Windsor was the sexy star of the successful *Carry On* films, while Wilfred Bramble was regularly seen on television as *Albert Steptoe* in the BBC comedy series *Steptoe and Son*. Ronald Fraser, Melvyn Hayes, Davy Kaye and Bernard Cribbins were also well known comedy actors. More serious actors were Corin Redgrave of the famous Redgrave acting dynasty, and up and coming young actress Francesca Annis. The story revolved around the comic exploits of a gang of crooks who fled to Cornwall after a bank robbery in London. Disguised as monks they hid out in a disused monastery off the Cornish coast. Wilfred Bramble's character occupied a cottage at Sunny Corner on the outskirts of the village. The film was described as *"a small cut above the Carry Ons"*.

The Director of *Crooks in Cloisters*, Gordon Scott, would remember Portloe many years later when asked to produce a film for the Children's Film Foundation. When asked about locations he is reported as saying, "I know the very place." and so he brought his crew back to Portloe to film *Haunters of the Deep*. Made in the mid 1980's it tells the tale of ghostly goings on in an under sea tin mine with children getting trapped in the mine workings as it gets flooded by sea water. They are helped in their search to find a way out by the 'spriggans', the ghosts and spirits of the mine. Portloe and The Jacka doubled up as a mining and fishing village of the North Cornish coast.

Shortly after this sequences for a television film were shot around Portloe and Portholland. Starring Frank Finlay and titled *The Secret State* it told the story of an MI5 agent who retires to Cornwall only for his past to catch up with him.

1991 saw a major television production staged in Portloe, Broom Parc and other nearby locations. An adaptation of Mary Wesley's *The Camomile Lawn* with Sir Peter Hall directing brought many stars to the village. The cast included Paul Eddington, Felicity Kendal, Virginia McKenna, Clair Bloom, Richard Johnson, Tara Fitzgerald and Jennifer Ehle. Filmed for Channel 4 it involved many local people as extras, some when the cove became wartime Penzance for the day. Local boats were used in the scenes with villager Greg Spears having the unenviable role of playing a dead German pilot dragged behind a fishing boat. While filming one scene Joey Trudgeon was waiting with others in his boat Olga a short distance off the sea wall. Provided with a hand-held radio he waited for his cue. The Director radioed inviting Joey to communicate with, "Come in Joe". Responding literally, Joey put down the radio, started his engine and came in!

For those of us not used to the world of filming it was fascinating to watch the professionals at work, and to be surprised at how long everything took! While filming the harbour scenes it was as if the Director had a God-like control. When it was pointed out to him that the tide was ebbing fast I am sure I heard him say, "Don't worry, we'll control the sea!"

The imposing cliff-top house of Broom Parc, west of Portloe near Camels, was used extensively. Weeks of filming took place inside, in the gardens and on the adjacent coastal footpath. Local farmer John Rounsevell provided a field where the actors, and an army of technical staff, could be fed and rested. In addition he leant Sarah, a Guernsey cow, which had to enter Broom Parc house! In a later scene many locals were extras at a wake, while the area was scoured to find vehicles of the war era. The production when serialised on television raised a few eyebrows over the nudity and bad language. But it certainly brought visitors to Portloe in search of the stunning locations.

2002 brought a BBC unit to make a series called *The Wild West*. Written by Simon Nye, the author of the highly successful *Men Behaving Badly*, it starred Dawn French as Post-mistress of St Gweep. Portloe and its harbour were used to represent this fictional Cornish village, creating a false pub frontage and a prefabricated shop. Filming tended to be concentrated within a few weeks and once again involved villagers as extras. Some controversy reigned, especially in the local press, as to whether the Cornish were being ridiculed by the story lines. Some points were raised to good effect but perhaps the most common reaction was that it did not live up to its comedy label. The BBC however were confident enough to film a second series in 2003, which when shown failed to improve upon the first. The characters were once again too broad and too eccentric to be believable.

The construction of the 'pier' in 1959. All ages of Portloe's population pose for the camera. The young lady is especially placed!

THE COASTAL FOOTPATH

Although the South West Coast Path is a relatively modern phenomenon with the 594 miles from Minehead to Poole being completed within the last twenty years the need to walk the coast goes back centuries. Not walking for pleasure but with other motives in mind the coastal dweller needed to reach vantage points to observe fish movements, especially the migrating pilchards. Small hidden coves had to be accessed for 'wrecking' to retrieve much valued 'gifts of the sea'. Smugglers too would obviously avoid the main beaches and coves, and in their wake came the Coastguard patrols treading the paths and frequently daubing marker stones with whitewash. As smuggling activity decreased so too did the number of cliff-walking Coastguards with a resulting increase in plant growth.

Advice to ramblers was even given as early as 1885 when writing of Portloe's paths an alternative to the weary was '*if the pedestrian has had enough of the coast he can hire a vehicle to take him to Grampound Road Station. (7/- inclusive of Driver's fee).*' (1) A great deal of money then and an indication of who might then walk the coastal paths.

Hockin, walking in the 1930's found the paths on both sides of Portloe to be almost impenetrable. '*I did once try to discover that lost path (Portloe to West Portholland) – the original coastguard one – from the Portloe end one broiling midsummer day, and although I cannot recommend the attempt to serious walkers I shall not easily forget it. After an hour of tunnelling through bracken, often head high, and scraping bare-legged, through thorn bushes, brambles, gorse and nettles, it took me to a delightful but dead end on Caragloose Point. My experience underlined in my mind two important points: first, that the coastguard paths of Veryan Bay should be forgotten: second that the risk of getting cut off by the tide among the unchartered reefs and recesses of this intractable coast ought always to be remembered.*' (2).

To the west of Portloe things appeared much the same. Hockin preferred to use the road through Sunny Corner to reach Broom Parc where he comments, '*I have heard that one may use the Broome (sic) Parc drive; but there is no reputable path beyond; Pennare is, or has been, forbidden on account of the impudent selfishness of motorists; and thus the west side of Veryan Bay is even more difficult than the east.'* (3).

Walkers now have the luxury of the path being trimmed by the Council or The National Trust with signs being erected to guide their way through any ambiguity. Many detailed guides are available with advice being offered on each section's challenge. Compare Hockin's advice with that of Le Messurier in a modern walker's guidebook. '*The shattered craggy buttress of Hartriza Point (between Portloe and West Portholland) is crossed. Like Nare Head and The Jacka it is composed of igneous rock, but this is the only obstacle to easy progress.'* (4).

The coastal footpath is enjoyed by thousands each year. Serious walkers who march long distances, head down in all weathers with an arduous schedule to keep. We sometimes wonder whether some of the 'route marchers' have time to appreciate the beauty and wildlife around them. "Look, a school of dolphins!" we might inform. "Can't stop to look, got to make Gorran by dark." might be the reply. Many of the walkers are short-course ramblers often arranging drop-offs and pick-ups or devising circular excursions. Many a car is parked at Broom Parc for the short circular walk to include a break for refreshment at The Ship Inn. For Portloe the coastal path is a valuable contributor to its economy with the pub, hotel, post-office shop and café especially benefiting.

(1) Ward & Baddeley, *Thorough Guide, S. Devon and S. Cornwall,* Dulau, 1885
(2) J. R. A. Hockin, *Walking in Cornwall,* Alexander MacLehose, 1936
(3) J. R. A. Hockin
(4) B Le Messurier, *South West Coast Path (Falmouth to Exmouth),* Aurum, 1990

The Second Home

Be within sight, sound or a sniff of the sea and there you will find the second home. Less will you find the residence of a man for whom the sea provides a living, but more for a man whose living is or was in some far-flung city. A village lucky enough to have developed in beautiful surroundings because of a need to house the people who scraped a living from the sea or the land around it is now a village where such people can rarely afford to dwell. Tiny, rough and ill equipped houses that would have seen large families raised generation after generation have now become quaint cottages desirable with microwave and shower where infant cries or mothers' soothing words in gentle Cornish accents are seldom heard.

The second home however is not a modern phenomenon. By 1926, according to Veryan Parish Council the need to provide houses for the working classes was acute '*since a large number of houses are being used as*

Portloe in the mid 1950's. Now over 50% of the properties are second homes *summer residences and houses are urgently needed by fishermen.'* (1). As in many other Cornish coastal communities the only available building sites were those away from the coves and harbours; and because of the typical Cornish topography this meant building houses near or on the top of hills. In Portloe council houses were built in three stages between 1928 and 1950 on the former allotment site, a good ten minutes up-hill walk from the sea. Just what the hard working fisherman needed at the end of a long day!

The high demand for a second home in a desirable location has always inflated house prices, and as a consequence put the properties out of reach of most local people, especially the younger generation.

Occupation of the second home is usually confined to the summer months so that the resident innkeeper or shopkeeper has to struggle for more than six months of the year. Long gone are the days of Portloe's two inns, two shops and many other services. The Post Office survives by diversifying to meet the needs of the visitor, as does The Ship Inn by hoping for a good summer's trade to help reduce the winter's overdraft.

Portloe has had to accept the inevitability of the summer residences and indeed has made many long term regulars very welcome as adopted villagers. Of course the more frequent their habitation the more welcome they are!

(1) C North, *The Parish of Veryan*, Veryan Parochial Church Council, 1996

SUBSCRIBERS

Cornwall Library Service

J. Burley
Lena Wheeler
Peter & Madeline Cumming
Ray Bell
Jeanette Bell
Jack Bell
Alice Bell
Mr. & Mrs. Adam Whitehead
B. Turner
John Leach
Joyce Gilbert
L. G. Rule
John Rule
W. Rule
Janet Sampson
John & Mary Earp
Andrew Tregunna
Carrie Breach & Andy Wren
Mr. & Mrs. R. Foley
Mr. & Mrs. M. B. Owen
Ian, Pam & Thomas Wright
Martyn Lister
Richard Elliot
Margaret Misset
Peter & Sally Trussell
Mike Rawling
Mike & Jackie Trevivian
Kath & Cyril Powell
B. Penney
Marlene & Dave Sowden
Bill Dingle
F. Kufel
T. Kufel
Richard & Sheila Dasent
Roger & Kate Mutton
Ann & Denis Johns
Kate Johns
Caroline Johns
Mary Pratt
T. A. Roberts
Alice Baker
John Roberts
Mrs. D. Ball
Derek & Jennifer Jenkins
P. Butt
Jeanette Blamey
N. & P. Jones
Keith & Nicola Guy
Megan & Nigel Pearce
Steve & Karen Pell
S. Nicholls
Steve Stephens
Gordon Langman
Margaret Watts (nee Johns)
Sue & Geoff Burns
Anita Burns
Gena Mlynski
Lindsay Corr

Jean Buer (nee Bullen)
Noretta Bullen (nee Trudgeon)
Sue & Graham Harrison
Tom Harrison
Bryony Harrison
Jan Smith
Hartley & Marjorie Everett
Viv Pascoe
Marian Sharps
V. Blamey
R. A. Hughes
Maureen & Ivan Ursell
John & Vanessa Richards
Ellen Richards
Mary Twiss
Alan Garthwaite
Vick & Lin Murray
D. & S. Malyon
Lawrence Malyon
Charles Malyon
Eleanor Malyon
Ted Arthur
Clare Holdsworth
Mr. & Mrs. Merrylees
Lee Johns
Clide Tregunna
Mark & Patsy Cotton
Jerry Charter
Horace Nicholls
E. Ruse (nee Johns)
Sam Rickard
David & Valerie Goodrich
Gerald & Joan Morse
John Dennes
Alison Gibb
Pat Rowe
Colin & Lin Rees
C. Humphries
P. Noble
Leslie Clarke
Ralph Clarke
Alison J. Lang
Hilda & Colin Powell
Robert Schofield
Joy Lamb
Ken Rainbow
Barry Rainbow
Fletcher Nicholson
Joanne Hillestad
M. Smith
John & Marilyn Wheeler
Mike Richards
Ben Johns
Barry Tregunna
Rafe & Clare Cotton
David I. Foster